HAPPY FAMILIES

To Pat –

All good wishes,

Joan Clifford

Summer 1991

HAPPY FAMILIES
By Joan Clifford

Fount

An Imprint of HarperCollins *Publishers*

First published in Great Britain in 1991 by
Fount Paperbacks, an imprint of HarperCollins
Religious, part of the HarperCollins Publishing Group
77–85 Fulham Palace Road, London W6 8JB

Copyright © 1991 by Joan Clifford

Printed and bound in Great Britain by HarperCollins
Manufacturing, Glasgow

CONDITIONS OF SALE

Introduction and Acknowledgement

As will become evident from the following stories, I believe in the value of the family as understood from Christian teaching – a life together for husband, wife and one or more children. I believe in the mutual responsibility of the spouses to care for one another and for their children and other relatives, and ideally to bring their children up in the knowledge of the Gospel, understanding something of the love of the Christian God for them. I believe that parents, on offering their children for Christian baptism, should want to make their own promises and try to walk the Christian way along with their children. I believe that a sense of unity and caring should flow over to the extended family and continue throughout life.

I do not believe that accomplishing this is easy. That it is not is borne out, obviously, by the growing number of family breakdowns. Moreover, the ideal of the Christian family is in itself under threat as being only one of a number of relational options.

I believe that the ordinary, normal family unit, particularly within the resources of the Christian Faith, is at its best remarkably powerful and effective. There is within it a marvellous elasticity of tolerance, patience, pride, support, unselfishness, learning and sheer delight and fun. The family unit at its best is also amazingly absorbent of sorrow, disappointment, error, shame and tragedy.

Where are these wonderful families? When I mentioned to a friend that I was writing about "Happy Families", he replied cynically – "Are there any?" Well, I did not have to search all that far for a group of families who seemed to me to answer my definitions. They look like anybody else and would certainly have reservations at being called "ideal". They have known problems like any other family . . . they have made errors of judgement . . . included unhappy members . . . have not known all the answers to awkward relationships . . . have gone through awful troughs as well as great highs . . . felt at times like disowning the whole pack. Yet all have testified to the predominating joy and sense of rightness at being a family unit, and have placed this high above other joys.

Of course, simply having united parents and loved children does not ensure permanent unshadowed happiness. A family I have known, where some members were high in public life, constantly experienced the embarrassment of seeing their son's name in the newspapers on demeaning charges; another family worries all the time at their daughter's inability to maintain a stable relationship; sometimes, where there are extended family commitments, the tensions between the generations are extreme. Things are not invariably easy; there are irritations, troubles and hard memories.

Yet when asked about happy family experiences, these have quickly come tumbling out. It is not easy to present these impressively. As with writing about "good people" in general, there is a simplicity that eschews the dramatic. Can there be anything exciting about an ordinary family Christmas, a christening party, the day Bobby gained the scholarship or a place in the team? What is interesting to others about that long-sought reconciliation, the reunion with those overseas cousins, the celebration for the old folks, the moving at last into the new house, the job finally achieved? All these simple events are of interest mainly to those involved but they are universal and part of the cement that keeps the family unit strong. These elements are valuable, satisfying and cumulative. And in their specific ways, they are what gives each family its special identity.

There is something about "the family" that seems to be beyond definition and certainly beyond the sophisticated sneer. When I was a Junior Army Officer in World War II, I was struck by the strenuous attempts made by young soldiers, despite their "man of the world" airs, to get home for Christmas. Mam and Da suddenly became very important, sisters, nephews and nieces were to be reckoned with. Come what may, if they possibly could, they would struggle to get home for December the twenty-fifth. Only within the family were they truly accepted.

And so I am very grateful to the families who permitted me glimpses into their own happiness and allowed me to share it with other people. I hope their stories will prove encouraging to those who feel that family life has collapsed in Britain. I felt the strong sense of what it meant to belong in these families and a powerful spirit of togetherness. The families were very different – each with its own lifestyle – but among them all I was conscious of genuine affection and freedom in their social unit. And of course, for all of us in this book, family life goes on developing; we don't know what tomorrow will bring. True Christian tenderness is needed to infuse family life throughout and among the generations, and we need above all to recall that we are part of God's great family and never out of His loving hands.

As well as being enormously grateful to "my families", I also appreciate the help of those who made introductions for me and opened valuable doors. These include Mrs Pat Snelling, Mr George Maguire, the Rev. George Thompson Brake, Lt. Col. (Ret'd) Ralph Nye and Padre Ross Peart.

I also acknowledge, in respect of the chapter "The Hampton Family", the valuable information contained in their book *A Family Outing in Africa*, by Charles and Janie Hampton and their Children (Mac-Millan 1988).

Joan Clifford

CONTENTS

I can say yes –
Joan Clifford

I am very glad to express my own appreciation of happy family life, for I have been and am much blessed. My childhood home was open and hospitable. Numerous relatives, friends and acquaintances of all ages were constant visitors, and we were expected to be tolerant of and courteous to the "odd bods" so often drawn in by my compassionate parents. My brother and I had agreeable grandparents and plenty of that diminishing commodity – The Aunt. Since our mother was quite often ill, we were thrown on the resources of relatives and took this for granted. An abundance of male cousins was uncommonly kind to a small chubby girl, so many years their junior. When visiting them it was my task to carry the maggots for the fishing and they, in their turn, would bash anyone who annoyed me. They continued to be affectionate and concerned, and when I later showed an interest in a theological student, afterwards to become my husband, they demanded, "Who is this preacher fellow our Joan's going around with?" Alas, so many of them have now left this world but they were very much part of my happy childhood.

We revelled in the huge family Christmases when uncles sang slightly risqué songs and were in one breath admonished and encouraged. Our father, in his fine bass voice, declared "Drake is going west, lad", and our mother, after her customary urging, sang emotionally in her deep contralto "Friend O' Mine . . ." Charades, when uncles dressed up and could hardly be identified, were rather frightening. Even more frightening was the epileptic fit perpetrated by an elderly in-law one Christmas morning, to be followed by the catching on fire of the turkey. . . .

How absurd and insignificant are the incidents of which most family life is composed; the awful jokes, such as our father's inevitable eyebrow-raising response to the appearance of custard-sauce: "Everybody mind the bones!" Likewise the silly nicknames that haunt you to the end . . . Porky, Squibs, Babs, Bonny. . . .

Our father was a big, handsome man of many talents. He was artistic, an above-average fast bowler, a lover of good literature and, like many of his generation, an inveterate spouter of verse. He would burst into gobbets of Shakespeare, as for example, if we were late for breakfast, declaring with Jacques: "'tis but one hour since it was nine and after one hour more 'twill be eleven." The most useful of his aphorisms, which continues to come to mind in times of crisis, was a line from *The Cloister and the Hearth*, where the hero is given to bellowing "*Courage! Le Diable est mort!*"

More important, father was honourable, warmhearted, sociable and popular, well-contented with a life bounded by his office, his cricket club, his home and his church. To all he gave his utmost, to the point of scrupulosity. He was fun to be with, a man without enemies.

Yet he depended much for confidence on our mother, a small fiery woman, unsuitably named Lily, known to him as Ladybird. She once told me she could not see what he had seen in her, but when well she was vivacious, quite funny and fiercely loyal. She had an uncompromising attitude to life, and not for nothing was she a Nonconformist in her religious profession. She and I had many a verbal tussle but were not often seriously at loggerheads.

Sundays in our Christian home were indeed special days. No shop was ever entered, no ordinary work carried out. But we sensed no hardship, though we went back and forth to church in an organized and regular way. We did wear "Sunday best", and I enjoyed the opportunity to wear chic hats and to cast a speculative eye from the choir-stalls over the attractive young men in the congregation. Before leaving for church our father, ever immaculate, would inspect our shoes to see that they were clean and shiny.

Our church was as familiar to me as home. As well as benefiting from choral singing and giving solos, I learned to stand up in public without embarrassment and "give a paper", which led later to my being accepted as a Methodist Local Preacher, and I learned to work with a variety of people. This was in addition to receiving the tenets of the Christian Faith according to my denomination, and feeling generally very much at home therein, and developing a personal commitment to Christ and the Church which became increasingly important to me.

We often entertained on Sundays but were frequently taken, as children, to visit our maternal grandparents in their tall Victorian house in a pleasant square. There were strict routines for these visits, but though proscribed they were enjoyable in a quiet way. I recall the popping gas mantles in that old house, and the manner in which Sunday afternoon tea was brought up numerous stairs to the first-floor parlour, on endless trays, from the dark kitchen regions below. "Tea" included caraway-seed cake, the only cake, according to our mother, that Grandma had ever been known to make.

My brother and I then had two options. We could play the ancient piano with its twanging response to fumbling fingers, or we could read, sitting on the prickly horsehair sofa. We usually chose the latter, though the books were somewhat restricted. There were tear-jerkers like *The Wide, Wide World* in which Ellen burst our crying on every page. Much better were the issues of Arthur Mee's *Children's Encyclopaedia*. Best of all was a publication called *Living London*, in heavy binders, especially the issue devoted to London by Night. Since we had the impression from our parents that nearly everything that took place after ten o'clock at night was evil, we were naturally fascinated by this volume. I recall the vivid description of the great presses roaring and the delivery of the newspapers. It was another world and we were lost in it.

After leaving home to join the Women's Services in World War II, I naturally saw less and less of my parents and my brother, especially since later my husband's job was itinerant. But when, during the last two years of her life, my mother came to live with us, we found a new kind of companionship, more relaxed through our greater experience of life. She continued to treat me rather as a child, worrying if I was a minute "late", but she made a true new life for herself and entered into strong new friendships.

When, well over eighty, she had a massive coronary attack and was taken down the road to the local hospital, her words to me have proved enduring. Though my husband had been incredibly kind to her, and I felt I had done my best, I was rather conscious of having sometimes been impatient with her. She now said, in clear tones, "If I don't come back, I've been very happy here." It can never be easy to join the generations together, but her remark made it all worthwhile for me. And perhaps her last words to me, uttered with her usual spirit in the ambulance, remind us of what family life is so often all about . . . absurd things . . . everyday things. . . . "You naughty girl!" she chided with a twinkle, whispering into my fifty-year-old ears . . . "You've let me come without my teeth!" Alas, she needed these no more as she died that night.

The open house that was so much part of my parents' lifestyle was echoed, I hope and believe, in the Manses shared by my husband and me for forty years, and by our son for eighteen years. It is not always easy for children of the Manse; strangely, people expect quite a lot from them. Nor do some Manse wives relish the rather rootless itinerant ministry of our denomination. Leaving behind people you have grown to think of as dear friends can be painful. I can only say that I have enjoyed meeting so many different people in the various parts of the country to which we have been sent, and have found the role of the Minister's wife, as I saw it for me, very creative and worthwhile. Congregations, I think, are pretty patient . . . There are lots of great memories and one is proud and humble to have been admitted so closely into people's lives, particularly into their personal joys and sorrows. We were often under financial stress but never lacked anything really essential, and we always managed to have some kind of holiday.

The old metaphor that "life is a journey" is specially true of our denomination, and now that we are retired that part of our journey is over. And of course the young bird flew the coop many years ago. I do not think he always found it ideal to be "the preacher's kid", but I sense that he has been proud of his father's work and he himself certainly grew up possessing very definite standards of his own.

When you are continually beginning again in new places, it is ideal to be close, to support one another amid the bewildering temporary strangeness, and this I think we were and did. I certainly believe there is likely to be greater happiness when husband and wife and children are of one heart and mind in the dedicated life which was our privileged vocation.

Now that this part of our life is behind us we find it inappropriate to use the word "retired". The two of us find new absorbing experiences all the time, having made fine new friends, and are simply thankful to have been spared up to now for several years of this "bonus" life, which is quite arduous. Yes, we are sentimental; we still remember and celebrate birthdays and anniversaries; the daft, tender things we write on cards are still true for us. And we both think the best times of all are when we are invaded by our son, his lovely Chinese wife and our two grandsons. Our home then comes alive in a special way . . . there is nothing quite like it. We thank God for our happy home life and pray it may continue for as long as possible.

Variety

What a variety there is among happy families — a variety of lifestyle and temperament. . . . One family's relaxed living is another's frightful muddle. One family's perfect holiday is the Costa del Sol, another's the Scottish Highlands. People make their own well-defined nests and want to live in their own specific way. There seems to be no norm for happy families except that of loving and caring. I have seen plenty of this, expressed in the old-fashioned virtues of unselfishness, patience and fierce loyalty. Our differing lifestyles give richness to life. Here are three different families. . . .

Ready for Anything – The Hampton family

When all together they are a formidable unit, the Hamptons. Yet totally appealing. Some might say they engage in crazy undertakings; the fact is, they are ready for anything.

Their home, a place free from obvious tensions, tells you a lot. It speaks of the creative mother, Janie, attractively thirtyish, and the practical, dark-haired, smiling father, Charlie. Also very definitely of the three young Hamptons, independent, individual, open – all with their mother's golden-auburn hair. Theirs is a house of many modest-sized rooms with sufficient space and privacy for all, giving an impression of light, colour, activity. Here is a large wooden figure with a dotty flowerpot hat; here the most striking paintings; here a white piano open, with music scattered about. Guitars and trumpets stand in corners. Here is a photograph of one child with a young black friend, heads thrown back in laughter under an African waterfall. There are souvenirs from African days and bold posters giving information on matters of social hygiene. These are probably intended for overseas use but are stuck unembarrassingly on walls around the house. Each child's room overflows with evidence of hobbies, concerns, delights. There is nothing anonymous here.

Janie displays with pride Charlie's household skills. Here he has put in extra showers and converted this and that; here is the extra bathroom with underwater-pattern tiling. "It's even more romantic if you bath by candlelight", says Janie. And beyond the house she points to the neat garden, orderly and productive: "Just a mass of weeds before Charlie took it in hand." Charlie's shed or hideaway is peacefully situated at the end of the garden.

This home speaks of a family with few hang-ups — social, reliigious or racial. It is a family that finds the world a fascinating place and is ready to do anything, go anywhere, meet anyone. It is a family with a strong social conscience which it works out in happy ways.

Just at the moment, all five are "here", but one gets the feeling that at any moment they may all be somewhere else, thousands of miles away. Janie is heard to mention that she will "probably be off to Baghdad for UNICEF on Monday". Nobody turns a hair. They seem to hold loosely to convention, but implicit in their lifestyle is a firm sense of true family, of unity, of belonging together and standing together before the world.

Both parents are from quite large families. Janie is from a family-tree going back to the Gurneys of Norfolk, a distinguished Quaker family. From her mother, the writer Verily Anderson, she inherits one of her creative gifts and is an author. Her books on health care and sex education are written especially for the African market. Charlie was a humanities tutor for the

Open University before going to teach in St Augustine's Mission in Penhalonga, Zimbabwe. With their children, Daisy, Orlando and Joseph, they wrote together their delightful book *A Family Outing in Africa*, and they were finalists in the *Sunday Times* Travel Competition in 1986.

In 1980 they left England to live in Zimbabwe, and while Charlie taught economics to ex-freedom fighters, Janie edited a magazine for the Ministry of Health. They adapted well to their new life and rapidly made friends around them.

Five years later they made a decision to undertake what looked like being an exciting trip, which they enshrined in their combined book. They would journey through Central Africa. This trip was to take them through Zambia, Zaire, along the Trans-African Highway; then to the Rift Valley and via Rwanda and Uganda to Kenya and to Nairobi. During this trip, when young Joseph was only six years old, they carried no more than a rucksack, and travelled in limited comfort by bus, train, river boat, lorry, wooden bicycle and on foot. Differing African lifestyles opened up before them, sometimes delighting them, sometimes depressing them, sometimes astonishing them. They were frustrated on meeting the celebrated pygmies of the Ituri forest, whose only means of communication was laughter; they were thrilled to meet the gorillas in the corner of Rwanda, Uganda and Zaire. Remembering to be slow and gentle on encountering these, they were rewarded by a view of the great silverback Mulifi and of baby Kampagna. "Seeing them was a real privilege." The family met gold-panners and handsome young Masai warriors in blood-red robes.

They stayed with consuls and with missionaries and, indeed, developed strong feelings at the attempts of some missionaries to obliterate the various African cultures. They could not believe that this is always a good thing to do. Sometimes, they believe, we try to alter the culture of people whose own is already truly harmonious. Yet the Hamptons gladly acknowledge their own Christian commitment, and Charlie has recently spent time as a lay pastor at a local Anglican church in the university city where they presently live. Their criticisms of some forms of missionary activity arise from what they have observed during their travels. The young people could not understand the "whites only" swimming pool attached to one mission. "It's really weird", said Orlando. But all the Hamptons readily acknowledge the hospitality and help and friendship of various missionary acquaintances during their journeys. They visited churches and also clinics and hospitals where they could.

Of course there were memorable moments during their African adventure. On Lake Nakuru they saw thousands of pink flamingoes. They went for a moonlight sail in a small dhow in the Indian Ocean. On the edge of the Rift Valley they glimpsed volcanoes. And they saw the romantic Ruwenzori – the "Mountains of the Moon".

There were also some ghastly moments when the parents experienced doubt at having brought their children into dangerous situations. One such occurred when their overloaded truck, making its way down an escarpment, tried to pass a stationary vehicle. The driver hugged the inside of each bend, then it was "grind to a stop, slip forward, stop again, then without further warning, a tumbling of freight barrels, the sound of screams and broken glass". The lorry turned completely over. Charlie and Janie managed to scramble out and began searching frantically for the children. Daisy was pinned under an oil drum, but after some heaving, she was out. Orlando was hanging upside down, startled and in pain. Charlie worked feverishly to get him out. Then to find little Joseph, in his David Livingstone hat made by Janie from a torn pair of trousers. His name was embroidered in red on the front. Where was he? In the ensuing panic, was he screaming or was he too silent? To their immense relief, they came upon him, trapped across his waist and ankles, letting them know how he felt! Thank God, they were able to extricate him.

They got clear of the accident scene and took shelter for the night in Rutshuru. Then an awful reaction set in. Should they have been there at all? Should they have been more scrupulous in making the driver check tyres, etc.? But they were all alive. Charlie found a furniture factory and ordered crutches to be made for Orlando, who was soon hobbling purposefully about. They were all bruised and shocked and felt they had been near to death. But soon they recovered health and spirits and went on with their tour.

The Hampton family is like most – sometimes in concord, sometimes not. During their travels they were often tired, hungry, really weary after awful journeys. Usually these feelings did not last for long, and there were ways to let off steam. When the African children cheekily taunted them as they trundled through villages, the young Hamptons would enjoyably shout rude things, knowing they would not be understood. And there was a lot of family fun – including the children's complaint about Dad's smelly feet and a combined threat to make him buy new socks. As well as their own games, they would join in with the African children they met, in wooden bicycle races or in Tzoro, a game with pebbles and complicated rules. And there was the day when Orlando was given a crocodile – over a metre long – for his birthday, something unlikely to happen in England.

The children did sometimes become weary of walking and had to be threatened that if they didn't hurry up they would be left behind. But if the travelling became really tough, Mum would help matters along by describing the stupendous and terrifying journeys she had read about in the *Geographical Magazine*.

Janie could be in trouble too. She made the mistake in Goma of arbitrarily pointing her camera and taking a flash in the darkness of an overcrowded lorry, beneath the tarpaulin. At once a man seized her by the arm and shouted, "How dare you! This is my woman. Did you ask permission?" Things got a bit angry. Charlie came to the rescue. "Please accept my apologies for my stupid wife," he intoned, "she doesn't know what she's doing. I think the camera went off by mistake. How can one see in the dark?" The angry man subsided. "Why should we concern ourselves with the foolish creatures? You are my friend. . . ."

The affection of the Hampton children for their parents is transparent. "She's a great Mum", says Daisy, smiling. Of course they have some things to complain of. Asked if he could do most things round the house if necessary, Orlando nods. "I always make my own breakfast – Mum doesn't like to get up early." He grins and tries to look injured. And asked if, in their family circle, the so-called modern practice existed of the whole family talking things over, Orlando mumbles something to the effect that "we might all talk – but we know who really decides things . . ."

Back in England for the moment, the Hamptons are living a fairly traditional life for the time being, but there is the sense that life is an adventure and who knows where it will take them next . . .?

Finding a Family –
Sylvia and Edward

Two little girls play happily together in a comfortable living room. One is very fair in hair and complexion; the other has a totally Latin look, with dark hair and eyes. To the world they are the sisters Vivien and Chloe, and people may say, without giving it a thought, "they are not much alike". The girls do not, in fact, share the same genes. They are adopted. To their parents they are "a sort of miracle" since they came into the family home – till then childless – when hope of a family had been almost abandoned.

The joy which the two little girls have brought came after a lot of disappointment, familiar to many childless couples. The young parents had wanted children, and after waiting for some time after marriage and failing to conceive, began to be dispirited. They went through all the usual medical checks and were told there was no reason why they should not be parents. Much advice and many tests followed, to no avail. As Edward says, "In one's relationship, one began to think in terms of 'failure' and of apportioning 'blame' – and of saying 'whose fault is it?' It was not a happy development."

At last they decided they were not going to conceive and began to think of adopting. Much advice was received, some useful, some not. Edward and Sylvia wrote for appropriate literature, studied it all carefully and began to make application for a child. They wrote numerous letters and received disappointing replies. "No, forget it", seemed to be the theme. It was suggested they might consider the adoption of a handicapped child, but they did not feel this was for them. One society was less dismissive than the others, and suggested they should write again later. This they did and were eventually listed as "potential adopters". Then began the gruelling interviews, forms and questions. They responded to all of these and felt turned inside out. Though they conceded this was right, in order to protect the child, it was exhausting and in some ways rather demoralizing, since it began to make them feel inadequate.

Suddenly, to their joy, the day came when they received a letter to say that a baby was available. They had a strange mixed feeling as they hurried off to see the child. Both find it hard to describe how they felt on first seeing the baby, a beautiful little girl with a completely Latin look, dark shining eyes and hair. They met the young mother, which could have proved a most painful moment, but although the child had to be taken away from its natural mother, Sylvia says "the circumstances were not sordid or awful; the young mother just could not cope. But we agreed to her wish that the baby should be told of her adoption in appropriate time. And the mother stressed her wish that the child should be told her father was 'a fine man'. We agreed to all of this."

The baby did not come to Sylvia and Edward straight away, but first had a short stay with a foster mother. Consequently she was at first very disturbed – she was five months old – and took a time to settle down. She was named Vivien, and became now very Sylvia-orientated, naturally wanting to stay close to her mother. "This took quite a time to adjust", says Sylvia. "Vivien was about two and a half before she could relate with ease to other people. Very understandable." She then bonded closely to Sylvia. Now about seven and a half, the little girl is composed and very outgoing, a sparkling child, speaking easily of her adoption, and she likes nothing better than to hear from Edward the story of how she was chosen and brought home and made one with her new family.

Time passed and the family yet seemed incomplete, and Sylvia and Edward made a further application for another child. In due time Chloe appeared in their midst, blonde, placid, more philosophical, very different in looks and temperament from her sister, but fitting in easily. Vivien is most protective of Chloe.

This professional family was now very contented. Edward, a consulting engineer, has to make frequent visits abroad but has always been delighted to get back to his family and they rush to greet him. They felt able to increase their family again, and applied to be considered as parents of a third infant. Another tiny child came into this warm home but this time there was to be sadness and drama, indeed suffering. The natural mother of the child, within the legal time limits, asked to have her child back, and this had to be accepted. This was a moment of great pain for all, particularly it seemed for little Vivien, who clung to the new baby piteously and could not understand why she had to go away again. A sore moment, not easily forgotten. There was further sorrow for Sylvia, having at last, after all this time, conceived, then lost her own baby.

The family is now in calm waters, much enjoying their relationship with each other. "There is real excitement", says Sylvia, "in seeing how the children develop, with their own specific gifts and talents." The parents are intelligent and musical, and have much to offer their girls, but above all there is clearly much affection in this home. Discipline is broad and reasonable and based on the desire for all to be happy. "We think of the family as a place where we love one another and know each other very well and where all can give and all can take."

Family joys are private joys and have full meaning only to the people concerned. Simple pleasures are to be shared, enjoyed and remembered. "We had a lovely day on Vivien's birthday in the summer. She asked to be taken out for a meal and we drove to a restaurant for lunch, very grown up. Then we went to the National Trust beach, because Vivien revels in sand and Chloe is big enough to join in and made sandcastles. Then we all climbed the dunes and went home for tea. . . ." For this family, it was a perfect day.

Sylvia and Edward agree that the grandparents were understandably cautious at first in their reception of their new grandchildren. "But of course they succumbed totally on actually meeting the girls and now think there are absolutely none like them," smiles Sylvia, adding, "Some friends saw our happiness and followed suit!"

We're Very Busy Here! –
Richard and Jane Harris and Family

The church was filling rapidly. Many of those coming in were not recognized as church members. There were ripples of excitement. The flowers were bright and there was a general air of expectancy. Passers-by outside were curious – was it a wedding? Then car doors banged, the focus of interest had arrived. A special party of people, with just a little trepidation, went into the building. A very special christening party had arrived – Richard and Jane Harris with four-year-old Tamsin, plus the family's newest members – Lauren, David and Megan. The Harris triplets, believed to be the only ones in Derbyshire, had come to be baptized.

It was a great day for all. Family and friends assembled early, plus a group of people from the Chesterfield Royal Hospital who had looked after the babies in the special baby care unit. They looked proudly at one another, and with satisfaction and affection at the three tiny figures being carried forward. The babies were immaculately presented in long christening robes, all parts of a voluminous garment originally made by Richard's great-grandmother and which had been worn by Richard at his own baptism. Some of the congregation noted how the "family faces" appeared on the babies – two having "big round faces" and one rather longer. They noted that two of the babies appeared placid and peaceful while the third was a real "live wire", with arms and legs going like a miniature windmill. There were the customary "oohs" and "ahs" and mutters of "aren't they adorable!" The christening was recorded on video and no doubt will one day interest and amuse the triplets themselves. It was a day to remember for parents and family and friends alike.

This christening was more than a happy conventional celebration for the young Harris parents. They were both convinced Christians and lay preachers in their branch of the Christian church. Full of joy at their splendid gift of three children, they take seriously the promises made at the baptism and desire to fulfill them. One cannot be sentimental when three new babies arrive together into a home. Their upbringing is undeniably a task, though a joyful one.

Having survived the trauma of a premature birth, when the babies each weighed in at under four pounds, and two months in specialized hospital care, the children were brought home and a routine had to be established for their feeding and general care. Looking after one child is quite hard work, and when multiplied three times during the same period it can be very strenuous, especially if disturbed nights occur. It is obvious that the first few years of life for the parents of triplets are not going to be too restful. . . .

There are twins in the family, and Richard and Jane knew quite early on that triplets were expected. The waiting time would be one of joyful expectation and perhaps a little fear and worry. A father's responsibility suddenly for four children instead of one is quite heavy. No particular financial help is available for such big families, but a home-help does make life easier for Jane. Her own family is not so near but Richard's is nearby, and so family and friends help with "sitting" and in little ways relieve the busy parents. And Richard, says Jane, "is a splendid daddy who just dives in when there are jobs to be done. He can and will do anything for the babies."

Jane and Richard realize it is important to try to keep some personal life for themselves, and when the babies were still very young, a "respite break" of four days, when the babies went back to hospital, was much appreciated. The young parents continue their preaching studies and above all enjoy their private moments with their little family, watching them develop and grow.

Elder sister Tamsin now relates well to her brother and sisters. At first she was somewhat suspicious and slightly aggressive, but sees now that her place in the family is in no way diminished. She is very protective towards her siblings and proud of them.

Jane speaks seriously about the situation facing young mothers of babies who want to come to worship and have peace of mind. This is something to be solved with just one baby, let alone three. Is a crêche the answer? Will people grumble if the babies are in church and "make a noise"? Jane feels this is something all churches should face, if they want to encourage young families to attend.

Because of the immense care bestowed on their family during the birth and early baby days of the triplets, Jane and Richard are, not surprisingly, much involved in fund-raising for the special care baby unit at Chesterfield Royal Hospital, and have been able to draw their local church into this valuable enterprise too.

Richard Harris trained as a teacher and later became a businessman. He has for some time been thinking of offering as a candidate for the ordained ministry of his church, and is taking practical steps in this direction. If this all works out as he and Jane hope, it is more likely that the family will not have to worry unduly about space in the days to come, as the Manses in which such families live are usually spacious and sometimes enormous. So there should be plenty of room for four growing children and their belongings and activities. Plenty of room for hide and seek! And for the privacy that is essential at times in any family, however happy.

DECISIONS

One decision can make all the difference to the life of a family. Shall we emigrate? Shall we offer a home to Granny? Shall we sell the business? At some points we just must make up our minds. Here are four stories of families where a decision was crucial for their future. They all agree that they talked matters over very thoroughly with each other. Some made their decisions a matter of prayer. These families are happy with the choices they made and express no regrets.

Farewell to "The City" — Justin and Caroline Welby

Making a change from a well-settled existence and facing a different and demanding future needs thinking about. Justin and Caroline made such a decision and made it together.

This young married couple are emphatic that they talked things over together and came to their decision unanimously. This was that Justin should resign from his successful business career as Group Treasurer of a well-known oil company and seek to take Holy Orders. They followed this through, and to their delight Justin was accepted by the Church of England and is now going through his three-year theology degree course at a northern university and enjoying his studies. Husband and wife are genuinely delighted and quite at ease with the thought of the changed life before them.

The young couple and their three little children live in their tall, pleasant Victorian house, living not in opulence but in quiet comfort. Their home is orderly but in no way fussy. Yes, they like to be together. Justin did not at all like the idea of leaving Caroline and the children in their former home during his three years of study. He accepted that sometimes married students benefit less from college life than those living in, but is of the opinion that he has the best of all worlds. He sees his family and is able to take his share in their upbringing, and at the same time his roomy spacious home is also ideal as a venue for visiting students and groups, who are offered open house.

The Welby parents have much to offer the established church. They are a personable couple with good education and social experience. After schooling at Eton, Justin went up to Cambridge, where he met Caroline. At first he began reading Law, intending to pursue a career at the Bar. But one day he suddenly thought, as he pondered some abstruse point, "Why am I doing this? I don't really care about it . . . It has nothing to do with anything that is really important to me." And that was the end of Law.

After leaving Cambridge Justin went into business and was successful. He admits to having enjoyed his business life, particularly the travelling involved, which took him to Europe, the Far East and Africa, where he was obviously observant of all that he saw. He would seem to have good social skills; he is a member of a large extended family; and he gives the impression that he would neither waste time himself nor value time-wasters. There is a lot of charm but also an element of sharpness and authority.

Justin and Caroline married, and Justin became a family man, and Caroline, a thoughtful and caring mother. She is a poised and self-possessed young woman, serious but with a charming smile and a pleasant speaking voice, moving calmly and purposefully within her domain. In their large, welcoming kitchen she attends quietly to the baby and offers to guests her delectable home-made brown bread. At the meal, Justin says grace.

It might well have turned out that their professional life, which one supposes could easily have been labelled "yuppy" at this stage, would continue to their retirement, with Justin accepting increased responsibility with ease and Caroline acting as a graceful hostess and getting involved in various charity roles. But suddenly it changed.

What led Justin to reconsider his lifestyle as and when he did? His decision to offer his life to the Church originated, he thinks, during his time at Cambridge. He was listening to an American preacher speaking of his own call to ordination. Justin insists that there was no "blinding flash of inspiration" at this point, and indeed, as a calm rational person, seems to resist this idea. He had always been idealistic and supported the established Church. Yet there seems no doubt that this was the moment that acted as catalyst and sent Justin off with the seed in his heart and mind that would later develop into the challenge to a vocation within the Church. Once this seed grew, Justin sought to find opportunities for testing his service and for offering his personal gifts. He spent time as a helper at the famous church of Holy Trinity, Brompton, with its multifarious activities and impressive programme of spiritual and social events, finding a place within the pastoral opportunities offered here, and able to take a part in community work. He found that he was acceptable and happy doing this work.

When it came down to the details of application for Holy Orders, Justin and Caroline were a little amazed and sometimes amused at the careful probing and scrutiny of their lives and motives for wishing to enter the Church. There were enquiries to ensure that Justin was not "totally intellectual" but could come down to earth when necessary, and enter into the lives of less privileged people. The two young people themselves seem to have had no doubts at all on this score. "Justin can be quite practical", said his wife "and will deal with problems when they occur."

There were also efforts to make sure they realized that their worldly expectations would be minimized, and that there would be a considerable reduction in their income. The church authorities were anxious that Caroline in particular should understand this. Her reaction was that she had already accepted this aspect of her new life calmly and practically. "I have good friends among clergy wives", she said, "and I shall turn to them for advice." She agrees that there are certain basic requirements to be covered, such as good education for the children, but seems quite unworried. Justin and Caroline recognize that they are not quite in the position of very young candidates who have had no business experience or opportunity for making financial provision.

Speaking of his expectations for the future, Justin says he wishes to work in an inner-city church and is undaunted by the idea of doing this. He is a very bright young man and will obviously bring much to his vocation – not only financial acumen, but also a readiness to face intellectual difficulties and a keen concern that people should attend church services.

He is idealistic but not unrealistic – old enough to have seen something of life, a man of self-confidence and a sincere Christian faith. And in his pilgrimage he is blessed with a sympathetic wife, one who is with him in his new venture, and has been from the beginning. "We were of one mind", says Justin. They have not forgotten, nor ever will, a personal trauma they shared, a close family bereavement. "We are well-fused", he says, "we have been through things together and we are secure. If we had not made the decision we did, I'm sure we would have regretted it."

To a certain extent, Justin and Caroline have committed not only themselves but also Peter, Timothy and Catherine, to a different lifestyle. It is not always easy for children of the vicarage. But these children have parents with so much going for them that it would be hard to believe that an exciting, interest-filled, challenging life does not await them all. . . .

Together on the Croft –
Christina Sargent and Family

How many families dream of "leaving it all behind" and quitting the urban rat-race for less stressful pastures! And how many actually do anything about it? One family not only talked about this but actually made their dream a reality. Christina Sargent and her family came to rest on the Isle of South Ronaldsay, in the Orkneys, where they are to be found living and working on their organic croft, or small farm.

The seventy islands of the Orkneys are separated from the "top" of the Scottish mainland by the Pentland Firth, and the climate is mild. Islanders have always farmed and have a reputation for being go-ahead. The Orkneys are a great place for antiquities and have been occupied for about six thousand years. From stone-age people to Picts and Celtic priest-kings, to Romans and Vikings, to Stewart overlords, to Italian prisoners-of-war; they have now been joined by Christina Sargent and her family, who bring their own distinctive contribution.

Christina Sargent (her professional name) was formerly a professional musician, but the travelling life and the care of a child became very exhausting. She was not satisfied with life. Then she and her husband, Mike, who had both known earlier sad years, formed a

rural community to embody their ideas, but unfortunately this did not work out. Finally they made the
big decision and moved to the Orkneys, a place they
had come to love and which seemed to offer a solution
to some of their problems. Here they work extremely
hard and are not entirely cut off from the competitive
modern world, since they must be self-supporting, but
with their children and a motley collection of animals
they are happy and know greater peace of mind.

Christina works on the land with her husband, as has
always been a characteristic of Orkney women; old
illustrated books of last century even show the women
bent low under wicker baskets of seaweed fertiliser and
peat. The family grow their own vegetables on their
organic croft – without pesticides or chemical fertilizers
– and oats and hay for the animals. They find this
satisfying, though as Christina says, "It can be very
tough cutting field beans in a cold easterly gale!"

According to his wife, Mike can do anything, from
harvesting to re-roofing, underfloor heating and car
maintenance, and is "the loveliest father". He seems to
possess a quiet inner confidence that carries him forward. Christina has her own very special gifts, which
she has bent to commercial use. Having once worked
for a potter, she discovered tactile talents and has an
innate love of beauty. She now runs her own business,
designing and producing felt rugs, cushions and
covers, something which sprang from her fascination
with the unusual properties of wool. Using the fleeces

of local sheep, as she became familiar with the different varieties, she began to explore the ancient processes of felt-making. Some of the dark brown and white fleeces she dyed, using vegetable juices to give deep, rich colour. She has entire artistic freedom, and makes all her rugs and covers on her own, working in a converted byre joined to her kitchen.

"It is so beautiful", she says. "My windows look down to the sea and cliffs to the south and east. I've always needed to make things and loved rugs and cloth." She has become increasingly successful with her venture and has held an exhibition of her work in Edinburgh. She acknowledges her creative temperament which, as with most musical and artistic people, can lead to tension and rushes of nervous energy, and claims that Mike understands her very well and is a calming influence.

The family house itself is an inspiration, with its fine exposed stone and the bright covers within, made by Christina's hand. It is warm and cosy, and outside Mike is making a splendid sunken garden.

Life is never dull for this family. They also take visitors throughout the year, as their brochure says. "Life is full to bursting", confesses Christina. Added to their cheerful and varied existence on the croft are teenage Daniel and younger siblings Lorien and Islay. Also the Jersey cow and offspring, some milk sheep and assorted coloured pet sheep, numerous chicks and ducks and the old, well-travelled goose, Matilda.

Christina and Mike are idealistic in the modern manner, and strive to bring up their family according to their own standards. They feed them organic food and are generally conservation-minded. They naturally long for the best for their family. There is obviously much to delight children in this beautiful and exciting part of the world. Due to a discreet oil presence, there is work for young people, so the population is not dwindling. A good education is offered at the Kirkwall Grammar School, and many young people return to the islands to work, bringing their youthful vigour and forward-looking optimism.

And when the children are not in school, there is an enchanting freedom for them – Daniel likes to swim, to cycle, to make bows and arrows, and there is space and safety for young children, amid a lovely part of the country that must surely influence them.

The parents recognize that growing children will certainly have their own priorities as time passes, but these children have much love and security, as well as talented parents. Mike and Christina think they may not be very orthodox, but they do have a lot going for them in a busy life on their Scottish croft in Orkney, away from the hectic traffic-ridden bustle of the great cities.

"Moving" does not alter one's temperament, and Christina understands that there is continually the need to sort out life and to achieve a balance between hyper-activity and laissez-faire; nothing is ever totally simple. But she and Mike would certainly say that, in spite of setbacks and the hard work, their dream of a better life has come true.

Letting Dad Go –
The Barkers

"Short-term aid projects are no use", say many people, but the Barker family does not believe this. They proved their point by sending Keith, the father of the family, off to South America for two months. His return, obviously happy and fulfilled, has convinced them that they did the right thing.

It would be true to say that Keith, in his late forties, had made up his mind that he ought to go, but of course he talked it over with his family – wife Katrin and two sons, aged sixteen and nineteen. He emphasizes that the decision really was a family one, not easily made, but when he finally left for Bolivia, he went with family blessing.

His decision to take part in this project – "at his time of life", as his boys said from their youthful vantage point – arose from a contact with someone deeply involved in the Christian organization known as STEP – Short-term experience project – and in response to urgent need by the Evangelical Union of South America. He found himself deeply stirred by hearing of the struggles of a small group of Bolivian Christians to build a church for themselves.

Was the Lord calling him, in his mature years, to do something practical like this? Keith is a big man, fit, and trained as a mechanical engineer. Providentially,

Keith and Katrin had just sold their newsagent's business, feeling they would like a change, so there was no problem about Keith finding the time to go on this project. He also knew that he was in a position to make the considerable financial contribution with which the project must be underwritten – all members of the group paid for themselves.

Keith made tentative enquiries. He found that twelve young people were detailed to go to Bolivia, aged eighteen to twenty-three, and from a diversity of backgrounds, including a medical student. The STEP indicated that it would be delighted if Keith would act as co-leader with a young Spanish-speaking interpreter.

There was much to think about. Would he be able to relate satisfactorily to the young team? Well, he had been trained as a youth leader and had plenty of experience working with young people. He is a father of almost grown-up sons and a happy family man. "We've always been a close family", he says.

Katrin, a slim, pretty, silver-haired woman, herself very youthful looking, remembers their early family life. "When we first went into business our children were very young; it all worked out well. People said, "Oh, you were in business", but the children always knew exactly where we were and they grew up very happily." To help her in their busy life, friends took the young Barkers to the local Sunday School. This in turn led to the parents attending church to listen to them reading at special services. "And I was drawn into the ladies", says Katrin. "We soon became thoroughly at home in this church." The Barkers have always been on good terms with young people, and have grown increasingly committed to their church, particularly in its outreach.

Keith therefore perceived everything coming together as regards the Bolivian project. He had an inner conviction that he should go to help, both as a practical man, physically strong, and also as a father or elder brother figure to the younger group.

What remained to be discussed, he realized, was perhaps the most important: his family's reaction. Should he travel, even if only for two months, eight thousand miles away to a remote area, from which communication could be difficult, and leave a rather fragile wife and two sons? He was not just going on a short holiday. There could be difficulties – political instability; one would have to behave and speak very carefully; there were important matters of health and hygiene as well as language problems. Would it all work out or be merely a romantic dream?

The Barkers held a family conference and thrashed everything out. The boys did at first think it was a bit of a strange idea. "What do you want to go there for, Dad?" they asked. But they were sensible lads, well settled at school and in university, and with no special problems. There was primarily Katrin to consider. "We had never been separated in all the twenty-five years of our marriage", says Keith. But Katrin was amazingly strong about the whole issue and could amazingly strong about the whole issue and could sense that it was tremendously important to Keith to be free to join the project. By the time the discussions were over, the whole family had willingly agreed that Keith should go. The boys promised to "keep an eye on Mum" and, says their mother, were very caring. They were also, despite themselves, becoming interested in the project. So Keith signalled "Yes" to STEP and when the time came for the party to depart, he went with them.

Their destination was Potosi in Bolivia. All the party experienced culture-shock. Keith had lived for some years in Canada and was not untravelled, but he had not foreseen the extreme poverty of the Andean people whose lives he now joined. The South American republic of Bolivia has been called "the Andean land of snow and sunshine". It is very hot in the daytime but frosts occur each night. In this landlocked country the Bolivian people live in thatched mud huts on the high plateaux – Potosi is sixteen thousand feet above sea level, one of the highest towns in the world. From poor soil they scratch a living; barren soil and irregular rainfall make lives hard.

Despite extensive mineral resources the country and its people remain among the poorest in Latin America.

Princess Anne, visiting Bolivia for the Save the Children Fund, said later on a BBC radio programme that she had never seen such poverty. "You don't see people dying on the streets," says Keith, "but the level of life is so low." The Bolivian Christians, under their Pastor, Don Felipe, were so welcoming, the party knew at once that all would go well.

There was much to come to terms with for the party. They had to be careful about food – their young doctor was strict with them, forbidding dairy products and being specially severe about the water. You cannot boil the water, for because of the altitude it boils at only seventy degrees, and that does not then kill the bacteria. Three pressure cookers accompanied the party.

Keeping clean and sweet was a problem, especially for the girls. "Hygiene in the area is terrible", Keith wrote home. "There is no adequate water, people drink from the sewers, women sleep in what they've got on. They wash in the sewers and hang the cloths in the sun." Sometimes the party also had to drink from the sewers, and as protection, they put iodine into the gruesome liquid. Fortunately they had taken a good supply of drugs with them for medical use.

In spite of these and other difficulties, they soon established the happiest of relationships with the people of Potosi, and along with the Pastor began the task of building the church. They also did many little jobs – washing up, washing children, just generally sharing in the people's lives.

With the encouragement of Pastor Felipe, they got going on the building. They met each night for prayers and briefing. They had little or no experience in construction work, but the church was completed in six weeks, a church seventy feet long. It was built, mainly from materials at hand, by sheer manual labour, which was not helped by the altitude at which they worked. The girls and men dug and moulded about four thousand mud bricks, which baked hard in the sun. The roof timbers – corrugated iron and cement – were paid for by the Evangelical Union.

The emotional response of the people of Potosi confirmed Keith's belief that their coming was important. Yet he believes that the party received more than it gave. That very poor community taught them about real giving, though they themselves owned so little. On the first night in Potosi, before sleeping accommodation indoors had been sorted out, their sleep in a courtyard had been disturbed by the cold. Next night a group of local women brought rough blankets which they pressed on them, and they then slept warmly. Only afterwards did they discover that the blankets had been the women's personal bedcovers, and that these ladies had had to sleep huddled together to keep themselves warm. But this generosity had been prompted by the Bolivian Christians' understanding of New Testament attitudes.

The greatest inspiration was the Pastor, Don Felipe. A man of about forty, he had made himself a pastor through concern as to the depressed future he foresaw for his neighbours. There are extensive mineral resources in Bolivia, but world prices have plunged, and Pastor Felipe correctly foresaw the closing of the tin mines and the great wave of unemployment that lay ahead. He had "learned his Bible", as he would put it, and had decided to put his beliefs into action. He still gives his life to the evangelical Christians of Potosi and lives by faith. In the building of the church he was foremost, as pastor, foreman, plumber, builder. "He is a really great man", says Keith — "a great, loving Christian."

The church was finally raised and dedicated, a moving occasion. It was now time for the STEP party to leave this land of poverty yet of great beauty — a land of stunning mountain ranges where condors sweep through the heights, and vicunas, llamas and alpaca graze the land. A land where the people seem to have nothing. When Keith ventured to say this the Pastor smiled and shook his head. "Nothing!" he said — "Nothing! We have everything — we have Christ. . . ."

Back in England Keith was overflowing with joy and enthusiasm. The family received him back joyfully. They heard that the Potosi church was really being used, both as a worship centre and also as a community meeting place. Keith knew he had to inspire others to take an interest in Potosi, and needed no prompting to speak, lecture, show slides and appeal. "I can't forget that place", he said, and his local church helped him to fund a feeding station in Potosi, where there are so many orphaned and abandoned street children.

And what of his family? He has had no difficulty in enthusing them. "The boys seem quite keen to go themselves", he says with a smile. Katrin too is excited at the prospect of a project in which she and Keith can join together.

"As to the future, we don't know yet what God has in store for us", says Keith. "But it will be something interesting, bound to be. . . ." The Barkers did not really know what they were starting when they decided to let Dad go. . . .

The Wish to Heal – Alan and Pam

Three young men are "very green", say their parents. They have embraced vegetarianism and alternative medicine. The eldest did an A level project on an aspect of homoeopathy; the second son looks after his father's accounts; the youngest is also interested in the same field. It seems very likely that they have all been influenced by their father, Alan, a practising homoeopath, and by their mother, a woman of like mind.

The journey since marriage of Alan and Pam into an area of what they see as greater caring in society has involved a series of important decisions. The root of their progress was surely there when they met at teacher training in Cambridge – their Christian faith and its outworking. They did not know then where this would lead them.

Alan and Pam began their professional lives teaching modern languages, Alan in a public independent school. For some time they lived happily after their marriage, bringing high standards and much dedication to their educational vocations, and enjoying their own social activities. Both are gifted people with considerable presence. Alan early became a lay preacher within his church, and is musical, with a good voice. They are both good mixers, with attractive personalities.

56

As time passed three boys were born to them, and Pam conceded that for the moment she needed to be a full-time mother, although fully intending to return to teaching when appropriate.

Alan had become interested in counselling skills, and various influences had deepened this interest. A natural student, he attended a course of studies in lay pastoral care. Looking critically at his daily life he began to think of leaving the rather privileged educational circle in which he then moved and offering his skills in a setting where perhaps he could be of greater use. So he took a job in a community college where pastoral care could ease the transition of primary schoolchildren to higher levels of learning. This move was accomplished only after a family discussion. Pam had no objections, having decided that she could now start to plan for her own return to teaching.

With the new job came the inevitable home-moving, to Sussex, where they soon became part of the local scene. Pam began to build up a new teaching career, with forays into part-time and evening education. For Alan it was education with a somewhat different ethos but very satisfying. He began to be aware that he did possess some special counselling skills. Then, he says, "things began to happen". Wherever he turned, the "caring principle" seemed to rear its head. An inter-church committee held Lenten meetings, at one of which the need for a local counselling service was shown. This was surprisingly quickly established, and Alan later found himself acting as secretary. He now comments with pleasure that this organization is still going strong.

One day, in connection with overseeing a school trip abroad, a mother wrote a note saying that if her child were taken sick on the trip, she wished the child to be taken to a homoeopathic doctor. Alan admitted that he knew little of this system, which led the mother to advise him, very crisply, to find out more about homoeopathy for himself. So he began to do this, reading and enquiring and becoming more and more impressed. Shortly afterwards, quite coincidentally, he found himself listening to a talk by a practising homoeopath. "This was really my entry into the world of holistic medicine", he says. The basic principle of homoeopathy is the law of similars. It says that any substance which can cause symptoms when given to healthy people can help to heal those who are experiencing similar symptoms which are making them ill.

Happy as he was in his job, it now seemed time for Alan to make a career move to teaching a higher age range. Interviews did not seem productive, and it was all rather frustrating, until suddenly it occurred to Alan that what he was trying to do was not right for him. He was musing about this when Pam came straight out with it: "You're on the wrong track!

That's not what you really want to do: you really want to go in for homoeopathic medicine. . . ." Alan realized that this was true. It was the turning point.

By this time their third son was leaving babyhood behind, and Pam was re-establishing herself as a professional woman, and also as someone with a little more time to follow her own inclinations. She herself began to read and ask questions about homoeopathy, and they both began to question established medical practice. "It was rather a strange experience for us in our mid-thirties", she says, "but very exciting. I suppose it was really a quest for truth. . . ." They read, listened, asked questions, sought information. Finally they realized that they were in complete sympathy with the idea of homoeopathic practice and Alan began training in these skills.

Could he build up a practice of his own and make a satisfactory living for his wife and family? As was their custom, the whole family sat and talked it over, and the boys were extremely interested. It was eventually decided that Alan should make the break with his life as a teacher and try for this new profession, little knowing at this point that his teaching experience would also be valuable in the future.

The crunch came when Alan left his teaching post. There was the mortgage to pay, three healthy kids to look after, so Pam had to go back to full-time work, and it had to be immediately. They now went from one good salary plus Pam's smaller contribution from her part-time work, to one lesser salary. It was not going to be easy.

To work as a homoeopathic doctor one has to build up one's own practice. Advertising is not allowed, referral by word of mouth is the way to build up a reputation and a practice, and the beginning can be tough. Alan did have a disappointment in that he had been expecting to join an established practice with a friend – in fact a mentor – and to become a partner there. This did not work out, so he was on his own.

Pam now acknowledges that the beginning was not the worst bit. It was about two years later that the full weight of their reduced income fell on them. "Things did not build up as quickly as we had hoped, although Alan was doing well and building a solid name for himself." Pam found it hard going. Even an intelligent and thoughtful woman cannot make money stretch indefinitely without lowering standards. Shopping now required concentration, and holidays became times spent with parents instead of trips abroad. They were in no way desperate, but things were not easy and the parents grew rather weary. "I got very tired and fed-up", admits Pam freely. "It seemed to be all work for us then and I feel we nearly did give up."

Then Alan had a stroke of luck. He was invited by a publisher to translate and edit two books within his professional capacity, and this brought them some much-needed cash. It seemed another turning point. Next Alan began to teach for two days a week at the homoeopathic college where they needed someone with educational experience. At the same time the practice expanded more vigorously. Patients and friends would no doubt say that this is in some part a reflection of Alan's caring and friendly nature as well as his professional skills. Homoeopaths have always stressed the importance of assessing the totality of their patients. Alan himself was much happier and, says his wife, "he now looked ten years younger".

The decision to alter course in their mid-thirties has proved correct for Alan and Pam. Alan is now a registered homoeopath and is fully stretched in his practice. He has a sense of being greatly fulfilled and of serving society in a caring role. "I always had the wish to heal", he says. In all this he is totally supported by Pam, who is also once again making her own significant contribution as an excellent experienced modern languages teacher.

Alan continues to teach at the college and to work for two days each week at a clinic in Kent. His office is in his home, from which he also works. Asked if she objects, Pam says, "Not at all – the aroma of soothing oils is rather pleasant!"

This family went through a good deal of tough thinking and had to make some crucial decisions. On the whole it appears to have proved exhilarating rather than depressing as an experience, though Alan and Pam are both relieved the change-over period is past. Each is now well established in their personal careers, and now they watch with affection and great interest the futures of their three sons. They all seem to be happy, to be on the same wavelength.

Dynasty

Genealogy is now a popular interest but not many of us anticipate discovering that we are the scions of noble families; our interest exhibits curiosity rather than expectation. Is the fact of having a long ancestry in itself something to be proud of? Is there rather pride in the social value of the activities of some long-established families?

Some descendants feel a sense of obligation to their ancestors; they feel they must join the family firm or go into the Church – yet they do not truly want to.

But a sense of dynasty does inspire other people who are deeply motivated by the traditions of their families to take a part in the continuance of these traditions. Two such stories are told here.

All the Fun of the Fair –
The "Famous Thurstons"

"Where else could an old couple walk around, admiring the wonderful lighting, listening to the music, watching the people enjoying themselves, getting caught up in the fun and thrills – and all for nothing! And they can do this every night of the Fair!" Stanley, senior member of the great Thurston clan, chuckles. He is indicating the continuing fascination that the fairground has held from one generation to the next. And for those minded to spend, particularly the young, there are breathtaking new rides, familiar gallopers for the little ones, really spectacular lighting and the continual striving to compete in the world of today's sophisticated entertainment, while retaining the traditional favourites, the "joy rides" of old.

In early days fairs were held primarily to promote trade, and usually on a saint's day, as with St Giles's Fair at Oxford and St Valentine's Fair in Kings Lynn. The commercial side of fairs was gradually eclipsed by the attendance for amusement, and today the travelling showmen, mostly members of the Showmen's Guild, still crisscross the country on their "runs", offering fun for all. For over a hundred years great travelling families like the Thurstons have enabled the public to escape from the mundane world. The very names of the earliest machines were exciting. Who could resist the "Magic Switchback"? Who wouldn't want to go into the "Golden Dragon" with its superb organ, ornate waterfall and massive extension front which made you think you were walking into a magnificent palace? Whether it be a small street-fair or a huge, well-publicized traditional event, the fair still provides an hour or two in wonderland for all ages and classes of people.

And what of the travelling showmen who own and run the fairs? Are they enjoying themselves? They are certainly not escaping from reality, for the fairs are a serious business for them and more than a business — rather, a way of life.

There are several great fairground names, to be seen on headboards and on the sides of trailers, each of which travels with its own families from just before Eastertime to the end of the year, staying in winter quarters for the rest of the year. Even then there is plenty to do.

The Thurston "clan", with their winter quarters in the Amusement depot in Bedfordshire, consists of twenty-five families. The Thurstons are proud of a family tree going back in the business for about one hundred and fifty years. The founder of the travelling family was Henry, born in 1847. He had watched a rag and bone merchant utilizing a hand-operated children's roundabout mounted on a flat cart. This merchant was seen to urge the children to bring him rags in exchange for a free ride. Why should this unit not be operated commercially as an independent unit, thought Henry, and promptly went into business. He married the daughter of an owner of fairground equipment and the Thurston dynasty had begun.

Even when not blood-related, the various families, who live and work at close quarters, are linked together by their ancestry and way of life. They share a clan loyalty which binds them together and makes the fairs work. They may not always be in agreement but they support one another, particularly in times of trouble, and stand up for one another against all comers. In fact, they will support showmen of all families in the event of problems such as floods, broken axles, etc.

When young chaps and girls have been meeting and playing together since childhood outside the living wagons, it is not surprising that romance blooms and marriage follows. Such matches are likely to be stable and enduring, for the young couples will have much in common. They will be familiar with the kind of life before them and know what will be expected of them. They know it will involve much hard work but much reward too. Travelling showpeople work and play hard.

From boyhood, lads are learning the ways of the fair. They get used to the engines and machines, learning to keep them clean and bright, and how to repair them. "When I was a boy," says Stanley's twin brother John, "our father used to hand everyone a scrubbing brush and tell them to get cleaning." The fairground may seem a glamorous life but it means doing a bit of everything, turning your hand to anything. A showman must be practical, having to see to generators, engines, wiring, painting, metalwork, besides keeping up with new inventions and developments.

Girls too must be useful. They are sometimes away at school when young, as weekly boarders, but still have plenty of opportunity to pick up from their mothers the duties that will later be likely to be theirs. Schooling is now taken more seriously, and a real effort is made by most parents to see that their families benefit from education as much as possible. In their neat, comfortable caravan, Vera, Stanley's wife, describes how their daughter worked very hard and persisted to obtain a travelling teacher for a group of young children on site.

The girls know that a specific kind of life awaits them in the world of travelling showpeople if they marry. Such a wife has a lot to fit in, apart from caring for her husband, looking after the home – frequently on the move – and bearing children. Large families have always been welcome, for in a family business, every pair of hands helps. Then there are the duties especially of a fairground wife.

"There are really no hours", says Vera with a smile. "At the end of the day, you might have to make meals for any number of people who have been working on the showground. You may have to collect and count takings, take a turn in the pay-box, often be asked to give advice. You may have to speak sharply to the 'gaff lads' who work on the 'rides'. It is all part of the job."

While she talked, Vera was attending to several small grandchildren who ran in and out, delightedly greeting their grandparents and behaving like children anywhere.

"Discipline is sensible", says Stanley. "We say to our sons when they go out for the evening – don't take cigarettes from anyone, you could get into drugs; don't let go of your drinks, then they can't be spiked; and when you come home, tap on the window and let us know you're back. . . ." Such concern and palpable sense of togetherness helps to keep the community close and to keep trouble away.

The families have their problems, sometimes associated with the strange ideas people have about them. There may be difficulties with authorities at site, perhaps due to misunderstandings. There are problems with awful weather, which keeps people away. Even actual travelling nowadays is less easy, more hectic than in the clip-clopping olden days along uncrowded roads. And there are the problems of a bad press. "It's not unknown", says Stanley, "for the press to attribute carelessness to fairground people in the case of an accident when it has been nothing to do with us at all . . . this sort of bad publicity is a real disaster." The safety record of the fairgrounds under the banner of the Showmen's Guild is very good.

In spite of set-backs, showmen's families would not live in any other way. Very few leave the business to "go outside". And their celebrations are memorable. Wedding feasts are famed for their extensive guest lists and generosity. "And in November, when we're going to close for the year," says Vera, "we have a fellowship-do. It's a great party for everyone, where we really enjoy ourselves." And at the famous and truly glittering Showmen's Ball, held in a large London hotel, no expense is spared and the ladies look magnificent.

In Victorian days the life of the showman was precarious and sometimes violent. One man who really knew this from experience was Thomas Horne, a barker on the show front before settling in Leeds as a doorman at a waxworks show. Tom began to take an interest in religious matters and eventually offered for the Church and took Holy Orders. He was at one time Rector of Syresham, near Towcester, but soon made the fair grounds his life work. He understood the difficulties of the caravan dwellers and their problems with the local authorities. In the early nineteen-hundreds he formed the Showmen's Guild of Great Britain. For the showmen he organized a Christian mission, travelling more than twelve thousand miles a year. And nowadays, about five thousand showmen, self-employed, independent businessmen with their families, still travel, ninety-five per cent being members of the Guild. The Guild is a strong valuable organization, powerful and respected.

Within showmen's families, rites of passage are faithfully observed. Babies are baptized and there is a high obligation to attend travelling showmen's funerals, where the floral tributes are amazing. The departed are remembered in the World's Fair magazine, and families may pay respect in the form of a poem or a photograph.

Stanley and John Thurston, speaking no doubt for many other famous names among travelling showmen, make it clear that in spite of problems and competition, the wagons will continue to roll and the drill will continue: arrive, set up encampment, build the fair, attract custom from the town, pull down and leave – often within the space of a few days. They are most proud of the charity work they undertake, particularly on behalf of children. "We give great shows for needy children", says Stanley. "We give all our services. We don't always get much acknowledgement from the press for this, but we love doing it. . . ."

And all the while, throughout spring and summer, the fairs will go on giving people harmless amusement. Many older people saw their first "living pictures" at a Thurston travelling bioscope show. And most people have at some time had a ride on a Thurston roundabout. There is fun for the public and – for the travelling showmen and their families – fun and hard work. In the main they are happy families.

On the Move for God and the Queen – The Robinsons

Three generations of Robinsons have served the Armed Forces in different ways. Of the second generation, the Rev. Tom Robinson has recently retired from the Army Chaplaincy service. After more than twenty years in the department he has now resumed parish activity in Humberside, and is getting back into this traditional routine, with his lively, attractive wife Doreen, in his elegant rectory.

As a boy Tom was already drawn by the Army ethos and was indeed an army son. His father, of Irish descent, who died when his boy was ten years old, had served in the Indian army and was one of the famous "Scouts". Tom's mother had spent some years travelling with her husband and was able to recount tales of the north-west frontier and exciting old times which must have seemed romantic to the young boy. "My father", says Tom, "was very knowledgeable about some of the native peoples and wrote accounts of their lives." The story of his father's service was an inspiration to young Tom, and it is not surprising that in due time the Army would also claim his allegiance.

Before that there were to be terms of apprenticeship and a widening of his sphere of service. As a young man, Tom had certainly intended to join the Army, but before doing anything about this he experienced an even stronger inner calling to offer for the Church. He is not quite sure how this came about, for there was no particular religious adherence in his family. However, the conviction continued to spur him on and he offered and was accepted for Holy Orders. He spent some time working with the Mission to Seamen, a valuable preparation for his later life as a chaplain.

He then, again under an inner conviction, fulfilled a desire to work in a rural Irish parish. "I always wanted to do this – probably because of my Irish ancestry – and I'm glad it was possible." He and his wife spent some happy time in a curacy there, but he admits that after a while he felt a lack of challenge and the need to look further afield for vocational satisfaction.

It came to him that there was a way in which to combine his calling as an ordained clergyman and also his admiration for the Army, so in 1966 he joined the Army as a Chaplain to the Forces, and during the following twenty years or so found a fulfilling existence. With his wife he entered on a challenging lifestyle that was to take him on many different tours of duty – in England, to Northern Ireland, to Germany – according to service requirements.

Tom seems to have settled naturally into army regimes and found no problem in the dual allegiance to the Church and to the military life. His own background made it simpler for him to accept military discipline and the ordered life of the Army, while he welcomed his new clerical opportunities within the different postings. "The moving about", he says, "was just part of being in the Army. It is not that difficult; one moves into similar situations and may well find people whom you already know when you arrive. There is no real problem; everyone knows their job and it is all very straightforward."

Having left behind her life as a curate's wife, Doreen too embarked on this itinerant existence, bringing its own duties and concerns. "Our job", she says, "was to make a home in the accommodation provided and to try to give it that personal touch." She understood the feelings of the young army wives — some very young indeed — when they arrived in their somewhat bare regulation accommodation, so much like everyone else's! She sympathized with their urgent need to do something to break the uniformity. "And there were the inventories to deal with — when you came and when you go — everything to be accounted for."

Sometimes the young wives were homesick and had to be coaxed out into social life. "If the girls were seen to be out and about, chatting, gossiping and generally enjoying a normal life, there was nothing to worry about", says Doreen, "but if we hadn't seem them and there were signs that they were shutting themselves away and brooding, then we had to try to do something about this and get to know them and see if we could help."

Overseas, within the rather self-contained Army life, people can sometimes see too much of each other; life can be rather proscribed. Because there is no real need to be able to speak the language of the foreign country, you can feel a sense of isolation, and there are sometimes rather frightening intermittent periods of particular political tension to cope with.

Doreen is an accomplished hostess with warm and graceful social skills and a kind heart, and has no doubt valuably complemented the work of her chaplain husband. She must have listened to many confidences in her years in service life, and is both sympathetic and sensible. She understands well one of the important decisions the Army couples overseas have to make concerning the education of their children – should they be educated locally or sent home to boarding school? "This is quite a problem", admits Doreen. "I have seen quite a few tear-stained faces of mothers whose children have gone away, though I don't suppose it lasts long with either the mothers or the children, but it is painful at the time . . .'." She thinks it is a difficult decision to make, and is not herself very much in favour of boarding school, believing more in the value of the home environment.

As well as a grown-up daughter, Tom and Doreen have two grown-up sons out in the world, one of whom has followed his father into the military life. This young man, after Sandhurst, had determined to become a Line Officer, but is now taking training which will make greater use of his specialized academic gifts. Like his father, the young Lieutenant is proud to have spent time in Northern Ireland.

Both the Army and the Chaplaincy service have their special ethos which is not always easily understood by outsiders. Army families have a pride in their traditions which is quite marked. And the Chaplains, whose task is not easy in today's secular society, are proud to continue to care for service personnel as they have always done, and, when senior in their service, to care for the more junior chaplains. A wife who understands both the Army and the Chaplaincy is indeed a valuable helpmate.

Tom came to the point of retirement from his chaplaincy career, having become Deputy Chaplain General, and is very thrilled to have been awarded the C.B.E., following in the footsteps of his much-admired father who was also decorated by his Sovereign. An attractive photograph in the Robinson home showing Tom, gold-braided in full-dress uniform, with his wife outside Buckingham Palace, will remind the family in years to come of the time in which Tom combined his devotion to the Army with his Christian commitment; years in which he exercised pastoral oversight, conducted worship and celebrated the sacraments, dealt with administration and attended major parades; years of travelling in which he and his wife undertook difficult and responsible but also exciting and happy duties for God and the Queen. There were sometimes periods of tension amid requirements to be alert to security considerations, such as having to look beneath the car before getting into it.

Now the Rev. and Mrs Robinson have severed this strand of their life and have returned to the traditional running of a Church of England parish. Doreen, a musical woman, is a fine organist and brings this special skill with her. And when it comes to "getting on with people" there is little one would expect to teach the Robinsons. In their comparatively modern church in a pleasant seaside town, they bring their experience and continuing sense of vocation to a further task. The future looks good for them and, if sometimes Tom becomes a little homesick for Army ways and Army talk, he will have the pleasure of conversation with his son, the third generation of military Robinsons.

Through the Mill

Most families go through difficult times, some more than others. It is unrealistic to portray family life as perfect, untouched by human problems. Many families have bad patches, others live permanently under disadvantage. There is often much suffering. Some are able to find, or be given, the resources to come through the darkness into the light. There are four such stories here. It so happens that all four acknowledge their Christian indebtedness and believe that their faith, either of long standing or newly acquired, sustained them as they went "through the mill".

Into the Sunshine —
Paul and Ann

A heady freedom can infuse newly-experienced university life. Paul felt this and revelled in it. Home had been great, and life in his well-attended local church had been fulfilling and enjoyable. There were friends in the youth club, and acting in church plays answered an inner need. But now, in this fresh environment, anything was possible. New friends invited him to join them in the local pub, where they were welcomed by the landlord and his wife, and by the local residents, who became a temporary family. With new studies and boundless drama opportunities, life unwound in an exciting way.

As time passed, acting consumed more of Paul's life; there was also much academic work to get through. Home and its discipline grew more remote. Sundays came and went; there seemed no time for church-going. He still went to church with his parents when he went home, but it dawned on him that his commitment, such as it was, had been more to the social life of the church than to his spiritual convictions. What did his parents think of his developing personality? Did they realize that he was by now an habitual drinker, and he from a totally-abstaining home?

A well-set-up young man, Paul soon met an attractive, intelligent girl and they believed themselves in love. His own traditional happy home had conditioned him to thinking that this was the pattern for normal people to follow. So they became engaged and before long married. In his heart Paul still yearned to be an actor, but had agreed with his parents that it was wise to get a degree first. Now there was an immediate need to make money and set up a home, and the acting had to be buried for the time being, so he went into teaching.

Cracks in the marriage soon revealed themselves. The young wife let it be known that she did not want children, and this "gnawed at him". Paul changed his job and went to work in a radio station where his duties as Education Producer were absorbing. Indeed they absorbed not merely a normal working day but most of his life. At home the atmosphere was deeply unhappy, and the marriage deteriorated. His wife, an academically bright young woman, was not herself fulfilled. By now Paul was drinking heavily. He accepts that he was in a bad way and his general health was very poor. He believed there was no future for his marriage, but held stubbornly to his wedding vow — "till death us do part".

Then he attended a big family gathering, and at the end of the evening found himself alone with his much-loved Father. The two men began to talk and Paul found himself opening his heart; all the misery and frustration tumbled from his lips. "Surely it has to be — till death us do part", he repeated to his father. There was a long silence. Then the older man said quietly but firmly — "Perhaps there is more than one kind of death. . . ." For his unhappy son this seemed to be a signal, a release from his own personal inhibition . . . at any rate, it was a turning point for him and he was not surprised to find that his wife also felt there was nothing further for them in their marriage. So this came to an end.

Paul came to know Ann, his present wife, whilst he was working on his radio station. Her father was a contributor on rural community matters and asked if any opening could be found in the programmes for Ann, a talented young woman. Shortly after, Ann won a prize in a competition for listeners' stories, and came to the studio to read her story. "She is a fine reader", says her husband proudly. "In fact, she is very creative, has a lot of talent; she can play the guitar, and sing. . . ."

Ann was also a bit lonely, and they found they had much in common. She was a firm Christian with a deep attachment to her local church and involvement in a lively youth group.

Paul and Ann married and began to know a quiet joy. But a personality that had suffered such upset as Paul had did not easily achieve balance. He was still drinking; it had become an obsession. He had previously undergone one period of treatment, but returning to the same unhappy situation and unhelpful surroundings had resulted in a relapse.

Ann says, "I remember a change in my attitude, a sort of strong determination that I wasn't going to continue having my life ruined through no fault of my own. I felt I owed myself that much dignity, and I said I was leaving – staying away until this drink problem was really tackled. It was the most difficult thing I have ever had to say and do but I stayed with it and left. Perhaps God was in that decision, I like to think that He was. I know I felt a sort of strength I'd not felt before."

Paul realized that this was a crisis and booked himself into a clinic – run, he says, by "wonderful people". Ann spoke to him several times during this period and sensed a greater determination in him. She says, "I returned home a day or two before he was admitted to the clinic. I saw him through the admission procedure and left him in their hands." Later, Paul attended therapy sessions and Ann accompanied him. She recalls, "I was also involved in some of the sessions, which gave me the opportunity to deal with some of my own deep feelings of anger and resentment. When Paul was discharged, the work really began for both of us. He had to work at strategies for overcoming problems and I had to work at re-building my trust in him. It was hard. But gradually I came to believe that there really was going to be a change."

Paul declares, "Alcoholism is a terrible thing. It is never cured but one can recover. . . ." And in all this mess he never forgets: "Ann came with me. . . ."

One afternoon, Paul and Ann and another couple went for an outing to the beautiful and historic city of Cambridge. The two young women went shopping, and the other fellow went off to look at books. Paul found himself sitting on a seat outside King's College chapel, idly watching the passers-by and listening to their various languages. He says, "Suddenly I realized I was feeling an unusual sense of peace and everything seemed tremendously clear – even the stonework of the buildings seemed crystal clear and shining." He found himself going into the chapel. It was not silent, for the place was as usual thronged with tourists and their murmurs. Hardly noticing, he sat down, and was flooded with an amazing new sense of confidence. He seemed to hear his own voice saying, "I don't care what happens now – it will be all right." He doesn't think he even knelt down, but he felt a different man. He went outside into the sunshine. Life began anew.

Paul now began to combine his two special interests – teaching and drama. Going to teach English at a big community college, he found himself developing a

department as Head of Drama. Everything was opening out. "It's amazing how you can move children
through drama – not just in their joy of using their
imaginations – you can reach the very core of them
spiritually and emotionally. . . ."

So he became fulfilled and happy in his work. At
home the same emotions enveloped him and his wife.
After a time of awful tension, unwinding gradually
followed. The drinking problem came under control
and they returned to the life of the church. He feels that
much of his recovery and spiritual return is due to the
prayers of others, particularly those of his parents and
of Ann.

"I have a very strong conviction of the power of
prayer," he says, "though I don't understand how it
works. But there is definitely a channel between God
and humankind."

Delightfully, the one gap in the lives of the pair was
now filled. The appearance of their baby son completed their happiness, and the day of his christening
and the great family party that followed was one of
incredible joy.

Paul now says, "It's easy to underestimate that
awful part of my life but it was a black, black time."
He recalls his father talking to him recently and saying,
"Well, old boy, things have really worked out for you
– there was a time when your mother and I thought
your drinking would kill you and we would be burying
you."

The joy of Paul and Ann continues in the closeness of their happy family. They are strong in their love for one another and their little boy, a source of continual wonder to them. They are also strong in the life of their local church, where both find a true spiritual base. Paul, using all his talents, is in training to become a local (lay) preacher, eager to pass on to others the Gospel of Christian hope, an experience to which he believes he can truly testify, for he has indeed travelled from darkness into the sunshine. And in another image Ann says, "We have climbed out of what seemed an impossible abyss."

She recalls the words of an old hymn which she copied into her journal during the dark days —

> I trace the rainbow through the rain
> and know the promise is not vain
> that morn shall tearless be. . . .

God Gives Us Strength to Cope –
The Crowe Family

"Come in!", said Stephen, smiling. He took the visitor's wet raincoat and indicated a seat by the fire. "Would you like a cup of tea?" This young man was welcoming and friendly to the visitor. To his parents and his brother and sister he has proved to be the catalyst in their lives.

Twenty-five years ago Ken and Barbara Crowe looked forward with pleasure to the arrival of their third child, to join children of four and two. The baby was overdue but finally arrived – a little boy. Barbara now says that when she looked at him on the first night of his life, she knew in her heart that he was "different" from the other babies. His tiny form displayed certain characteristics that prompted disquiet. Nothing was then said by the medical staff, and she tried to still her feelings. During the following six weeks, family and friends gave various opinions as to whether baby was "all right". But at the end of the six weeks the young parents were told by the consultant, not very skilfully, that baby Stephen was a mongol baby, that "he would never do anything" and that they might be advised to "put him away and forget about him".

Once known as mongols, Downs syndrome babies, the result of a genetic defect, are sometimes born to older parents, but can be born – as in the case of the

Crowes — "out of the blue" to younger parents. The life-span and the potential of such babies varies. Reactions to the births on the part of the parents are complex, but particularly bewildering when such a birth is totally unexpected.

Mothers and fathers experience a whole range of emotions – shock, anger, outrage, disgust, disappointment, a sense of being shattered at life. Some feel "guilty" and wonder if people will think "it is our fault". Some are sunk in self-pity but keep a bright social face in public. Some confess that their first thought was that the child might have been still-born, or catch a cold and die. Some are even tempted to end the baby's life. They think "How can we cope? . . . What about brothers and sisters? . . . What will everyone think?" There is a tremendous lot of suffering.

Gradually many parents then adapt, emerging from their intense grief to try to come to terms with the situation. But they want help, so as not to feel so dreadfully alone. Then follows a sense of adjustment. Not all parents can reach this stage, and some just do not feel able to keep the new baby, a judgement that must be theirs alone and ought not to be criticized.

Barbara and Ken Crowe, secure in deep mutual love, and a close Christian family, made their decision. They felt that God had sent them a very special child and that He would help them to care for him, and help Stephen to develop and fulfill his potential. They would try to see that he had the best kind of life possible. The decision taken, they set about making it happen.

There were a lot of early problems, practical things to cope with, such as feeding and sleeping. Stephen did not walk until four years old. But he developed slowly and their love for him grew. Looking after him consumed their energies and prayers. It proved hard at first to open their new lives to outsiders – they found it hurtful when people passed by in the streets, unwilling even to peep into the pram. Eventually Barbara found an acquaintance with a similar child and plucked up courage to make contact. A bond was formed. "You really need someone to talk to who truly understands."

But one day it was forced home to the Crowe parents that all was not well with their other children. The bright young son became withdrawn and uncommunicative, the little girl obstreperous and awkward. "I honestly cannot remember", says Barbara, "doing anything for them. I suppose I fed them and took them back and forth to school, but my whole attention was focused on Stephen." Harm was being done to the older children and something had to change.

After talking things over, Barbara and Ken called Jonathan and Debbie to them and explained that when Stephen was growing inside Barbara he hadn't been made in the same way that they had and would need a lot of help. "We asked them – would you like to help us to teach your brother? They said yes and took up the challenge." Barbara and Ken were thankful that the children had sent up their own cry – "Don't forget us! We need you too!" – and they proved to be the biggest teachers of all for young Stephen.

And so the years passed, years of struggle and achievement. There were pleasant and unpleasant experiences, tears and laughter. But the family unit remained strong. When the older children returned from some outing which could not encompass Stephen they always said, "It was nice, but we missed Stephen."

Jonathan and Debbie left school and took up professional training. For Stephen it was a matter of trial and error, successes in education and in work interwoven with periods of doubt and disappointment. Other people's attitudes did not always inspire Stephen with confidence. But he had his own personal triumphs and delights. At eighteen he made it clear that he wished to be publicly baptized within the Baptist church. He had always gone along to activities, and specially enjoyed playing the drums in the Boys' Brigade Band and in joining in the drill. He had always shown a sense of worship and a real awareness of the presence of Christ.

Their Minister agreed immediately that Stephen should be baptized by total immersion, as had been the other two young Crowes. Stephen wrote to each of his instructors at his Adult Training Centre and invited them to his baptism. To his joy they all responded and were deeply moved at the ceremony. As Stephen came up from the water he was heard to exclaim: "I did it! I've been baptized!" As a church member he brings his own warm personality and welcomes people to the church as a sidesman. The fellowship of the church is vital to him. The church may be the only normal community into which a Downs syndrome person is fully integrated.

At the moment, his parents do not feel that Stephen is fully stretched. He remains a responsibility, though an amazingly independent young man. He is still liable to disturbed nights, with breathing difficulties. He is still close to this brother and sister who, though now both married, live nearby.

Stephen's impact on the lives of his family has resulted in all four of them becoming professionally involved in helping-agencies. Ken and Barbara's early feelings of being alone also led them to become very involved in MENCAP, Ken going on to set up a branch of Mencap Homes Foundation which has now housed over sixty mentally-handicapped adults in their area. Barbara, together with a local doctor, set up a system of early counselling and group work for the parents of newly diagnosed babies, which became known nationally and internationally as the Southend Scheme, and when she is called to the maternity unit to sit at the bedside of a distressed couple she is able to say, "I know how you feel – we too have lived through this hurt. . . ." Ken and Barbara have valued the opportunities of putting their point of view, through the media, as advocates of better understanding of and opportunities for the mentally-handicapped.

When the family was invited to Buckingham Palace to witness Barbara receiving the MBE for her pioneering work, Stephen said, "I must come too for I'm the handicapped one", and he was right to remind them that without his coming into the family they would never have embarked on this kind of service.

Say the Crowes together: "We often wonder what we would have been doing if it hadn't been for Stephen. We can't stress enough how we believe God changed our whole lives round when He sent us our special child. We believe God has given us the strength to cope and we hope, in some measure, that we have been able to help other families in similar situations. We believe that God does work in mysterious ways but is always working His purpose out."

A Family Renewed –
Joe Whelan and Family

With glowing face Joe Whelan waves a file of letters. A neat, stocky fellow in his late forties, with true Irish colouring, he is humbly proud of these letters, testimonies to the help he has been able to give to prisoners and ex-prisoners. In association with the Langley Trust, and in ways he feels directly God-guided, he is able to say just the right words and make the right approach in circumstances of spiritual and practical need.

As Joe goes to greet prisoners when they leave prison, he knows exactly what he is talking about. He does "know how they feel", for he himself spent over twenty years in different prisons. Praise God, he says, for the new life he now leads, victorious over the criminal tendencies that held him in their grip for so long. And so he is convinced that he can offer new hope to others in the same boat.

Joe is a born-again Christian and this has made a complete difference to him and also to the family so dear to him. He is one of the blessed ones whose family has stayed close to him – a lovely wife and two fine children; a whole family for whom things have changed and for whom life has begun anew.

Joe finds it hard to explain why he alone of seven Irish children "went wrong". He realized early that his father had no affection for him and this dislike increased. The young lad was not long in a state of innocence – "at ten I was an expert liar". From nicking beer bottles and taking the cash tin, it was but a few steps to crime with the big boys. "My first nicking was at eleven." He found no welcome from his father, who was working in England; indeed his father untruthfully told him that the police were after him, so he quickly left his father's lodgings. "My Dad was always comparing me with my brother Eddie. When Eddie died, he said, 'Why couldn't it have been you!' I surely had a great chip on my shoulder, but this was hard to take."

Joe was "alone in the big smoke at fifteen". Soon he was arrested for fighting with a soldier and ended up "in the Scrubs – my first night in prison".

At twenty, in London, Joe got into the "jump-up" business (hijacking wagons). He now had plenty of money but confesses he was always afraid and lonely. For a while he ran a legitimate business pig-breeding, but the police discovered he was "illegal" and he was deported, all his stock and gear confiscated. Back in Ireland, there was no welcome for him at home. Back again to England. . . .

"I was nicked again and off to Manchester." It was back to defeat and degradation. "On this sentence I got on the wrong side of a big coloured guy, the prison bully. He tried to attack me one day in the workshop. I let him have it with a chisel and cut him real bad. I was charged with attempted murder, for he nearly did die . . . there was a seven-hour operation to save his life . . . he did recover. For me, more porridge, more Christmases inside. . . .

"I was deported once again, for taking lorry loads, for the attempted murder and for being illegal of course. I thought, blow this, I will have nowhere left to go, no one to turn to. I was a complete mess and spoiling the lives of so many other people. I appealed against deportation and went to Risley remand centre to wait for a decision. But I was sent back to Ireland. Mother was afraid to let me in — after all, I had threatened to wreck the place."

So Joe borrowed money from his brother Tom — who was glad to get rid of him — and skipped off to Jersey — "a robber's paradise in the seventies". Here he met a "lovely redhead" and set out to impress her. "She soon found out that I was a thief and kept giving me money to try to stop me. She was so good to me, even then." Thus Joe met the most important human being in his life, Carmel, a young Irishwomen then staying with her sister in Jersey. They began to look for a place of their own. They went over to Liverpool but soon Joe was back into crime. "I brought shame to Carmel and her family all the time", Joe shakes his head. Carmel was expecting a baby. They got married and later a fine son was born, young Joe. "He was a little cracker. I got them a nice house and bought

Carmel a St Bernard puppy. All went well for a while and then, bang, I was at it again.

"I was wanted for serious crime in Durham and charged there. Also Special Branch decided to try to charge me with being a courier for the IRA. I said, 'Rubbish, I should run a mile', but they wouldn't believe me. Everyone I wrote to had their home turned over and they photostated all my letters.

"I did time in Liverpool, and Carmel never missed a visit and always brought our little son to see me. She was great – she kept the home together, she wrote to solicitors, to governors, always my link with reality. When I came out I did a proper job for a while, then I was in trouble again. The CID came and searched my house and really frightened Carmel. She looked white and ghastly. 'Blimey,' I thought, 'I'm sick of this. They must think my house is a sub-station, they are there so much.' Poor Carmel said, 'Are they never going to leave you to live normally? It looks like they are after you for whatever goes wrong.'"

She gave birth to a lovely little girl. Her unusual name, Shallanta, was chosen by young Joe, who said God had put it into his mind. The name means "girl of peace" and, say her parents, she truly is. Joe said, "Now there are four of us to love one another."

One happy moment surfaced. Joe's parents asked to come from Ireland to meet their grandchildren. "All the badness I ever felt for them drained away when I saw just two old people – and I had made them old before their time, with worry, heartbreak, shame.

They were in time for Shallanta's christening. I was sad
when they went – it was my last chance to love them
and the closest I had ever been to my Dad. I told him I
was sorry for the way I had turned out. He said he was
sorry for never loving or helping me. Next time I saw
him he was dead – laid out in his coffin. I kissed him for
the first time in my life. . . ."

Yet Joe was soon back to crime. "I saw psychiatrists.
There were many rotten prison officers but others who
were good ones; they said, 'Joe, we never invited you
to come inside.' I was arrested again. In Risley, in
August 1983, I said goodbye once more to my wife,
and saw her face all strained and drawn from worry.
An Assistant Governor said, 'You are going to the
punishment block right away – we know all about you
– the police have given us a warning sheet.'

"The door slammed and I began walking up and
down . . . walking and smoking . . . smoking and
walking . . . nothing in the cell but a 'bed' made from
three planks of wood. I was crying in despair. I was too
old for more porridge and I was now ruining the lives
of my children as well as my wife. What could I do to
myself? I was utterly exhausted. I knelt down and
asked God to take me out of this mess. I had never
really prayed before. I cried bitter tears. I decided I
would never go near my family again – and how much
better off they'd be without me. At last I fell asleep."

"Bells woke me up – they test the alarm bells first thing. What was wrong with me? Was I going round the bend, cracking up? I hadn't had any drugs. Amazingly, I realized I did not have a care in the world. People, do you know where my God was that night? Not in some fancy church – no, Jesus was right there in that dark cold cell. Just waiting to come close, to forgive me, to take all my burdens and to judge me. Praise God, to choose me from the pit, the lowest of the low, and to lift me up. . . .

"When they opened up the cell they asked me why I was smiling. I said, 'Boss, I'm sure Jesus has helped me.' They locked me up again and brought a doctor. 'Staff, keep your eye on him – this is another of his tricks.' Yet the word is, I was happy. I can't explain it. My Jesus had done what all the doctors and psychiatrists could never do. Even the RC priest thought I was working my ticket to the Happy House, though he did bring me a Bible. 'You're not fooling anybody, Whelan!', called the staff. How wrong they were. Nobody could ever break me again. . . .

"Does that sound loony to you? In the security cell, with form as long as your arm, waiting to go up for all sorts of serious crime? Well, I'm telling you the truth. I felt like I had never done before and the feeling did not leave me. I had come out of the rubbish tip and I was walking through an orchard."

Joe began to read the Bible. He decided to make a statement, the first ever – "I wanted to clear my heart."

The Senior Medical Officer removed him to the hospital for observation. Here more strange things happened. He found himself giving away his tobacco — those terrible fights over "snout" — and the foul speech and awful lies began to fall away. Now he was put on the landing to help with the more seriously disturbed men. "They were really fierce, they would not think twice before attacking you, but they would take their medicine, do anything for me."

The prison doctor called him in. "You've really changed, Joe. You've done so much to help us. We will try to help you." But the judge ignored the doctor's report and gave Joe five years. "I did not even blink. I thought, 'If this is a test, Lord, then I've already passed. I've already found you.'"

In gaol it was distressing to see the problems facing Carmel and the children. Carmel had been astounded at the change in Joe, which she had first seen in his letters. But practical matters claimed her. They were desperate for coats, shoes, coal. She asked — "Shall I get in touch with your old friend?" "No," said Joe, "Jesus will look after us. Get rid of everything that came wrongly, everything rotten." "What about your clothes, Joe? Some you have never worn." "It does not matter — the guy who owned them is dead." Amazingly, all their needs were met.

Soon, in prison, Joe was able to claim that he had been filled with the Holy Spirit. "I have known gifts of healing, of being a channel for the Holy Spirit to reach more than twenty men. I have my own heavenly language, I have had wonderful responses to prayer." A senior staff member said, "Joe, you're making a mess of our records, from what you were to what you are!" Hardened cons asked Joe to pray for them, saying, "Joe, you're a real Christian." Hallelujah! What an honour!

Four years after Joe's release, his little house is festooned with congratulatory cards from Christian wellwishers. It is a comfortable house, everything in it new, gifts from friends. Also in it are four contented people. Carmel will never forget the terrible times of depression and insecurity — "I was always a private sort of person, never wanted to ask for help." The teenage children, young Joe now doing well at work and much respected by colleagues, nod quietly at the remembrance of bad and bewildering events of the past. Joe himself makes no excuses for that past. But overarching them all is the providence of God and the new life that enfolds them.

There is a spirit of hope and trust in this home. Joe is active in his new calling of evangelist, which emerged after a period of hard paid work. Carmel looks relaxed and happy and the young people are absorbed in growing up. "See what our Dad made", they say, pointing with pride to fine carpentry, to the newly-completed guitar. As Joe leaves the house for a meeting, they kiss affectionately and draw their visitor into a homely ring of prayer, as natural as breathing. The big dog and the tiny one jump up and down. It is a happy home, a family renewed.

Questions and Answers –
Tim and Diana and the Children

Why? – this could be the big question in the Whitney household. It could be asked by father, mother and all the children. It could be asked and it could be considered difficult to answer. But hard questions are not allowed to dominate their lives. The father of this family, Dr Tim Whitney, is a victim of the disability called muscular dystrophy. He has to live with this and so does his family – wife Diana and three teenage children. To an amazing extent they live a life rich in fulfilment.

Tim's disablement cannot be ignored. Since he was thirteen, muscle weakness has afflicted him, and the gradual development of the disease increasingly limits mobility. As a thoughtful Christian Tim has sought his own answers as to the place of his disability in God's plan. He accepts that suffering is one of the mysteries of life, and that there is much about life that is mysterious. But for him the Christian answer lies in Jesus, the cross and the resurrection. Tim has long since put his life into the hands of God and goes steadily on, filling each day with activity and interest.

Questions are very much part of his life, and not only within the family. He is Head of Religious Studies at a large sixth form college, with probably the biggest such department in the country. His students, aged sixteen to eighteen, are, as he says, at a critical stage in their development and full of views and opinions on everything. He engages with them in strenuous discussions, revelling in opportunities to probe with them the large and deep questions of life. Their youth and vitality seem to be a stimulus to Tim himself.

He is well equipped for his work. When studying theology he entered into the full training of a Baptist Minister. This training included pastoral studies and these have helped him immeasurably in understanding and relating to the vigorous young adults in his college life. He is well able to advise parents, teachers and youth workers on how to respond to young people's enquiries, and he does this effectively through the medium of the printed word. He is frank and clear as to how adults can best approach these questions: find out why the question is being asked (what really lies behind it); deal only with what is asked; always be honest in your answers, for children see through insincerity. Don't be ashamed to say "I don't know". He is ready to face questions of a theological nature, how to help children to know "what is right"; how to treat children when they do something "wrong"; and the question so important to little children – "My doggie has died – will it go to heaven?"

He makes it very clear that "he is very far from having found all the answers" but will not refuse to look at the questions and go deeply into them.

Diana and Tim have made a happy home for their own children and it seems that they do not puzzle too much about their father's disability. "My children have always known me disabled", says Tim. "I think they are hardly aware of the development of the disease." He supposes that this is why they so seldom ask the questions about muscular dystrophy that come so quickly to the minds and lips of adults. "Maybe", he says "they simply accept that they have a disabled father and get on with life." The matter-of-factness of the children is probably a relief. When they were younger they would comment that "Daddy has poorly muscles", and were totally accustomed to the ingenious method by which Tim could rise to his feet as required. A technically-minded friend had a brainwave, and an old vacuum cleaner motor was used to help bring Tim to his feet. But to the young Whitneys, Dad was simply Dad, a great father.

Tim observes that in the future they too may ask more questions, as the hereditary nature of muscular dystrophy impinges on their own lives and futures. There will be fears to be met and faced, especially as so little is really known about this disease. But this thought is not allowed to overwhelm the family. The concern of Tim and Diana is "that the young people come to their own faith in a loving heavenly father who desires only good for his creation."

Diana's is a busy caring life but she remains a calm, dignified woman, despite natural inner anxieties. She teaches part-time and often goes with Tim on his preaching appointments as a Supplementary Minister of the Baptist Church. She is very much his life-line. And Jonathan, Alexander and Anastasia are like children everywhere. To Tim the important factor in good family life is finding time for everyone – time to be together. Also, "Being accepting – taking people as they are."

Despite his professional activities and church duties, Tim has managed to get together and publish a book on his hobby of British postmarks. Profits and royalties from this go to the Muscular Dystrophy Research Fund. Tim and Diana are very concerned for the hundreds of people in Britain who suffer from the disease, and urge that funds for research are greatly needed. Most MD patients are young children who barely survive their teens, so as Tim and Diana say earnestly, "research is vital". This is a family with a wide, hopeful outlook, who have not allowed their own problems to dominate their lives.

In the Public Eye

Fame does not come to many of us and we do not know how we would deal with it. But we would probably strive to ensure that it benefited our family and did not harm them. An excess of public adulation can be difficult to handle and can be invasive of private life. Yet some people cope successfully with being in the limelight, and here are the stories of two popular media figures who believe they are managing to do that. . . .

Matching What I Have Had – Nerys Hughes and Family

The memory of her own stable and happy childhood is the basis for the family life of actress Nerys Hughes, her husband and children. This attractive and popular showbusiness personality is eager to confirm, as she has already confided to millions of radio listeners, that her own early days in Wales were "idyllic".

"My father was a local businessman and my mother stayed at home and looked after him, my sister and me. Mother was there to talk to when we came home from school and to be interested in all our doings." Nerys recalls evening walks by the sea with her father, and it is easy to imagine a laughing, dark-haired child bouncing along beside her Dad. And visiting various relatives who had farms engendered a love of the countryside. Family life was a contenting experience for the young Hughes daughters.

The local chapel also exerted a strong influence. Much is sometimes made of the repressive side of Welsh Methodism, but plainly it did not damage this bubbling personality. "We enjoyed our life at the chapel – not only Sundays, but also the social activities and of course we loved the outings." Several visits to chapel each Sunday do not seem to have proved too much, though she confesses that she thinks sermons were then too long, even for adults, let alone children.

But obviously the congregations were warm and accepting, and the general ambiance of girlhood religious training was relaxed and beneficial. She will not join with those who look back with shudders to early church-going days . . . it was a happy time for her. She has not lost her Christian attachments . . . "there are several preachers in the family and my nephew is now training for the ministry in Aberystwyth".

All this was quite some time ago. Despite her youthful appearance, Nerys says that she has "been in showbusiness for a good many years". During this time she has seen her career build into one of increasing success and popularity; her effervescent, cheery personality quickly attracts her audience to her. In a profession notorious for its volatile and fragile relationships, how does she manage to maintain a stable home life of her own today?

One answer is — it is not solely *her* home, but the home of Nerys and her husband, Patrick Turley. They work together to keep a good home life. This is not as straightforward for them as for some people, since their work takes each of them away for sometimes quite long periods of time. It needs thought and arranging.

"We try very hard", says Nerys, "not both to be away at the same time. It is not good for the kids. In fact, I get really fraught if this looks like happening and have refused work on this account. We really do try to make sure that one of us is at home for them." Nerys and Patrick have two children, a boy and a girl, now in their teens. No longer little, they still appreciate the presence and security of their parents. They are receiving a good education but will not be going to boarding school. As Nerys says, "The children do come first and we try to give them the love we ourselves experienced. I want to match what I have had in the way of total caring. . . ." In this she acknowledges the big part played by their housekeeper – "a lovely person".

Nerys is well aware that her name is familiar to most people, certainly to all television viewers. Fewer people not "in the business" know the name of her husband, Patrick. She says this is not any problem. Patrick is a film cameraman, successful at his job and well regarded among his peers. "We each do our own job and are good at it." Nerys is emphatic that the deep love she and Pat have for one another helps them to survive their separations and the pressures of the entertainment business.

How to handle fame so that the family has a private life is a pressure, but it does not seem to have overwhelmed the Turleys. They enjoy holidays together, either Spain, where they have a place – "and that's nice but it's not the complete answer, it's too far away for quick breaks" – or in France. They find France a delightful, restful venue, but even here people approach Nerys for her autograph. The children raise their eyes, but are used to this by now.

Autograph-seekers must be respected, says Nerys. "After all, they are your audiences." "Don't you get fed up with this?" I asked. "No, I remember what my mother used to say, that you should put yourself into the place of other people and they would be hurt if I refused. It is not a lot to do to sign your name . . . it pleases them."

Showbusiness folk are well-known for their generosity to charitable causes, and Nerys has chosen to associate herself particularly with one such charity that has a definite Christian basis, the National Children's Home. She is a much-loved and valued Vice-President of this organization, and graces various functions for them with charm and sincerity. She sometimes opens bazaars and garden parties and is an articulate young woman. She mixes easily, both with the organizers and with the public, and when her children were very small sometimes took them along with her. Someone involved in some of these occasions says thankfully, "She is no prima donna, very easy to work with and really gets involved."

Nerys herself puts it simply. "I don't do much but I'm proud to be doing it. The National Children's Home, for example is a very worthwhile set-up, they do a wonderful job. I am just trying to give back a little of all that I have myself received. I think I have the best of all possible worlds – a job I love and a wonderful family."

Nerys insists that she is "not glamorous". She says, "When I go out shopping I am just an ordinary local housewife." Although this may perhaps not be strictly true, it is true that like most ordinary families the Turleys try to be a close-knit private, happy family unit, and they seem to succeed pretty well.

Counting Our Blessings –
Alan Titchmarsh at Home

The word "family" is quite often on Alan's lips. Apart from his delight in his own family – wife Alison and two little girls – he speaks of the "good family feeling" at Pebble Mill, his television "home", and equally of the "family feeling" at the little village school which his daughters attend. Obviously "family" epitomizes "the best".

Alan recognizes that he is "a personality", with the advantages and problems that this brings. A bright-eyed, sociable man with a hearty laugh and an obvious enjoyment of life, he is a natural presenter and proved this early on when he was best known to the public as a gardening expert. Taking his knowledge to modest gardeners gave him pleasure, and he still regularly writes several gardening features.

After a spell in radio he moved to television, where he is now seen on the programme *Daytime Live* doing the thing he most enjoys – interviewing interesting people. He is not one of your "grey" interviewers, but a positive man to whom the interviewees can easily and quickly relate – lively, vivacious and friendly.

The Titchmarsh family is therefore not quite like all other people, in that they have a father whom most people recognize on sight. In the comfortable modern family home in Hampshire, with its steep landscaped garden and three great dogs alongside, family life is carefully guarded. In the company of his supportive wife – "my little rock" – and two doted-on-daughters, Alan enjoys the relaxation he requires in the midst of a fairly stressful public life.

These parents are determined to protect their girls from public exploitation. Apart from the occasional group photograph of the family, and attendance at some fête opening, their privacy is complete. And since public recognition came quite early to Alan, the little girls are accustomed to the fact that Daddy has a well-known face. They are used to their school friends saying casually, "Saw your Daddy on the telly". One small daughter, flicking through a gardening magazine in which she was used to seeing Daddy's pictures, was heard to ask innocently – "Where's the photo of my friend's Daddy?", naturally assuming that the fathers of her school friends would also have photos in the magazine.

The years of getting up at the crack of dawn for Alan are now thankfully past, but presenting "live" shows does get the adrenalin going. "I'm lucky to be doing a great job that I enjoy", he says. "I don't take it too seriously but you must take it seriously enough if you are supporting a family, and you must give it all you've got at the time." He thinks that the important thing is to know when to stop, and he hurries home to his haven in the family. "It takes a time to unwind", he says, and is thankful that Alison understands this. He pays an immense tribute to his wife: "She's always been great."

Alison is an articulate, creative woman, who was teaching dance when they met in the Barnes and Richmond Operatic Society.

"You've got to have someone supportive, but she doesn't necessarily need to join in", says Alan. "My wife isn't into gardens but she enjoys looking at and sitting in ours." He goes on, "I married my best friend. We have the same sense of humour and often collapse in the street laughing at the same silly things."

It becomes clear that Alison is more than a support to her husband and girls, very much a person in her own right. Still engaged in some dance teaching, and with an abiding interest in ballet, they attend performances together when they can. She says, "I sometimes wonder if our feet will ever touch the ground, but life is never dull."

There are activities at home that can involve all the family. They have built on to their house a small hall where they display historic theatre and ballet costumes, and where at Christmas they give charity concerts and sing carols for local people. The family likes to be together, swimming, riding or dancing. They enjoy holidays and Alan is enthusiastic about Italy, especially Tuscany. "Italians love children, don't they?" He remembers the delight of Italian diners on seeing the children coming in for a meal: "Ah, the bambini!" He is puzzled at the general restraint of the

British, and not only towards children, for it is sometimes hard work getting the British to loosen up, although it is something he is good at.

Getting people to be forthcoming is very important in the *Songs of Praise* programme for BBC television, where Alan is one of the most popular presenters. "I got into it sort of by accident," he smiles. A producer meeting him in the corridor and recognizing a successful communicator, called out, "Do you go to church, Alan?" On receiving the reply, "yes", the question came – "How would you like to present *Songs of Praise*?" Alan says that at first he was a bit hesitant, reluctant to appear "holier-than-thou", but then he reflected that this was an opportunity for witness. "I do go to church, I am a believer." Producers like a sense of commitment, and it would be bizarre, he thinks, for presenters of these programmes to be atheists or agnostics. So a visually splendid Harvest Festival was Number One for him.

He enjoys making these programmes, whether in tiny beautiful parish churches or in cathedrals with their magnificent organs. "It's great meeting all sorts of people and sharing a common faith." The hymns of course are those people choose, "But we notice more modern hymns now, especially selected by younger people." The interviews he conducts bring forward many interesting people, from whom he skilfully elicits their stories and their basic faith, and enables them to pass on to viewers what their Christian faith means to them.

"Sometimes I need a day off — a really quiet day. Maybe I potter in the garden and want to be left to myself", says Alan. Alison thinks, "He manages to keep in touch with reality even though he does move in starry circles. After all — he started life in the soil, and I sometimes think that's still where he's happiest. . . ."

Alan is emphatic. "From my point of view and Alison's too, the family is the most important thing. My career is enjoyable but my family comes first. With regard to the children, I accept that we have another ten years or so before they fly away and we want to make the most of that."

The two Titchmarsh daughters as yet seem to constitute no problems. "People keep telling me that they will come to an awkward age but it hasn't happened yet, and I hope that however they develop we shall always keep up a dialogue and never stop talking to one another. . . ." The Titchmarshes count their blessings, and are glad to be a happy family.

A Bit Different in Britain

We cannot speak of happy families without including the multi-racial families of Britain. Their lifestyle may sometimes be rather different, but love of and pride in their families is no less apparent. In fact the family unit and the extended family seem to count for more than in many of today's anglo-saxon English families, where ties seem looser and relationships more off-hand. For example, an Englishman married to a Chinese wife says: "We are not very sentimental, but there is a great emphasis on the serious contract we have made, to be loyal and to support and provide for one another. . . ."

It is not always easy for ethnic families in Britain, but many have made happy and dignified homes of which they and we should be proud. Here are two such stories.

Not Hiding Away –
The Family of Neelam Kurl

Twice yesterday the Social Services Practice Manager was in Conference. Today she greets her interviewer graciously, but at any moment she may need to answer the telephone or give advice or instruction, and her natural authority asserts itself. Now she turns to give her full attention, with a charming smile. She is probably a little different from her colleagues in adjoining offices. She is not wearing a skirt and sweater, or a trouser-suit. Instead she wears a graceful sari, because she is an Indian woman.

Neelam Kurl, originally from Delhi, is probably everyone's idea of an Indian woman at her most romantic – slender, with dark eyes and a long glossy plait of hair, and skin of the most smooth and fine sheen. She is also very intelligent and sits in her office for hours at a time at her professional duties, where she wishes to combine efficiency with warm-heartedness.

She is also a young wife and mother and happy to manage life on all these levels. Her husband is an Indian businessman, a world traveller, and she is accustomed to this. Her son, five-year-old Sanjay, attends a nursery school. His name, chosen with advice from the Hindu authority, is important to him.

Neelam is asked whether her husband objects to her being a professional woman. "Well," she replies with a

smile, "I was a professional woman when he met me."
She believes that among Asian people in England there
are many career girls, and that this may cause tensions
between young couples. "In India, where the old culture runs deep, one may expect certain things but in
this country our family structures are changing." It is
so, she believes, even with grandmothers who, in the
past, have been so important in Asian families in
coping with the grandchildren, to help working
daughters and daughters-in-law. "Nowadays, many
more women go out to work and not necessarily part-
time; they in their turn are not going to be the kind of
grandmothers who sit around. My own mother goes
out to work."

It is agreed that the care of the children is very
important, and Neelam admits that she and her husband are fortunate in being able financially to make
good arrangements for the care of young Sanjay when
he is not at school.

Neelam has lived in Britain since she was thirteen
years old, and seems to have settled calmly here. She
speaks highly of her comprehensive school in Bir-
mingham, which led on to University, and has no wish
to send little Sanjay to a private school. She met her
husband here. There are aspects of her marriage which
she knows are of considerable interest to white
Britons, but which she feels they do not really understand well. This is in the matter of "arranged mar-
riages", of which hers was one. She feels English
people have a picture of reluctant brides and grooms

being urged unwillingly to the altar, and having no say in the matter of their betrothal. "Certainly among present-day families in Asian Britain", she says, "it is much more a situation of introduction by the parents of the young couple to one another."

It seems reasonable to suppose that such parents would like to see their children married to someone from a similar social circle, with similar religious and cultural backgrounds and, in a perhaps more formal society, they would effect an introduction and thus facilitate matters. "If we disliked one another, things would go no further", emphasized Neelam.

There is a considerable ritual about Hindu weddings, with a great representation of the families and a lovely trousseau of saris for the bride.

Neelam believes that she and her husband and child do live a happy family life, although as she sensibly observes, "no family is happy all the time".

Neelam and her family are practising Hindus and try to observe religious festivals. She agrees that living in a multi-faith society in Britain does bring decision-time. Without wishing to be harsh with little Sanjay, she does not wish him, at Christmas time, to get drawn into "Father Christmas superstition". He is given some chocolates, which he loves, so that he does not feel totally deprived alongside other children, but for him presents are given at the Hindu Festival of Lights — Diwali — and in this way traditional beliefs can be preserved.

Not long ago Sanjay came home from school and asked his mother – "I'm English, aren't I?" Neelam says, "I replied – 'No, you are not English – you are an Indian boy.' I then explained the situation. I complimented him on his lovely, gorgeous skin. . . ." Sanjay thought about this for a while. He took a little convincing, deciding at first that he and his mother must be English, since they had fairer skins, and Daddy, with a slightly darker skin, must be Indian. Now, though, he seems to have accepted and understood that he is and remains a fine Indian boy.

"I do not want him to hide away", says Neelam, "he must be proud of his race and take his place among them." She hopes he will absorb family values, and thus is helped by having various Indian relatives not too far away.

Happy though she is living in Britain, Neelam is filled with emotion when she thinks about her extended family in India. She has not revisited Delhi for eight years, but recently a video was brought from India by a relative for her to witness a family celebration in her home town. "There were all my family! I had been away for a long time, but seeing that video – I was at once there with them all!"

Neelam mused over the Indian way in which extended families have lived under one roof, for better or worse thrust together. "It wouldn't be possible here," she laughs, "the houses just would not be big enough!"

Physical contact between relatives is rare in public, but hearts are warm, and the family is an important concept for Indian people. This is true of Neelam, her husband and little son as they make their homes in Britain. "I do not have a lot of leisure, I enjoy my work and work hard, and when I get home the three of us like to be together. We are a family. . . ."

Together –
Ossie and Megan

A public wedding brings its own excitement. Onlookers who have no connection with the bridal party press against the church railings from sheer curiosity and the old axiom that "everybody loves a bride". In 1963 quite a large crowd had gathered outside a country chapel, surprising for such a small place. Finally the doors opened and the organ pealed. There on the chapel steps were the happy couple, they and everyone around them truly wreathed in smiles. It was a moment for this quiet area to savour. There stood Ossie and Megan – the bride a slender, very English-looking young woman, fair-skinned and delicate, the bridegroom a well-set-up, smartly-clad black Trinidadian. Their mixed-race marriage had begun.

As they stood arm in arm, momentarily at the mercy of the photographers and well-wishers, it may well be that their thoughts were going back over the events which had led them to this moment of the joining of their lives. Megan would recall the day when, at work, she first saw the laughing, good-looking young Ossie, an able young man full of quiet confidence. She had immediately been drawn to him. And Ossie, who had come to England from his native Port of Spain, Trinidad, two years earlier, may have thought of how he had originally planned to stay in England for six months, but had still not yet returned. He was not then to know that he would never return there to live permanently. He had been much attracted by the sweet English girl. Ossie and Megan began to think of themselves as a couple, and knew they were falling deeply in love.

Megan would recall the moment when the respective parents were told of the intentions of the young pair to marry; they both knew theirs would be a somewhat unusual marriage at that time in England, and the parents would need to get used to the idea. Ossie had written to his parents and received back a kind letter from his mother. She had written with her usual affection but, reading between the lines, Ossie had perceived that she was asking him "if he really knew what he was doing", and was none too enthusiastic. However, she had gone on to say that if his mind was really made up, she and his father would give their blessing and wish the young couple well. Ossie had suggested to his fiancée that she might write a brief note to her future mother-in-law. Megan did this, explaining how much she and Ossie cared for one another and that she would do her utmost to make him a good wife. Megan received a nice letter in reply in which it was intimated – Megan says with a smile – that she was a lucky girl to be marrying Ossie!

The idea of the marriage was not so unexpected to Megan's mother, as she had already come to know and appreciate Ossie's fine qualities since he had been visiting her home and courting Megan.

So the young couple decided not to think of married life in terms of problems but to go ahead, and their marriage took place.

Ossie moved from his bachelor dwelling into the family home where Megan had been living with her widowed mother. Arrangements were made to afford privacy to the young couple, but it soon became evident that Megan's mother was a sick lady and needed nursing. In the early years of her marriage Megan devoted a good deal of time to looking after her mother, until the older lady moved into comfortable alternative accommodation, where she was happy.

The newlyweds settled blissfully into their new life. Ossie continued his career in telephony. There was no merging with the crowd in that locality, since there were and still are few black faces in the Fen villages. But Ossie saw no problems and made none. Some colleagues at work, who had known the two young people and wondered about the possibilities of the union, soon realized that the relationship was working well, and they gave little thought to Ossie and Megan's particular mixed marriage.

Ossie had never experienced difficulties in mixing with any company. He puts this down to his early life in Trinidad, where his father became Chief Inspector of Police. "All kinds of people passed through our open house", he says, "all races, all classes. I became totally accustomed to this." This attitude stood him in good stead when he came to this country and inevitably found himself in a racial minority. A calm, cheerful and confident disposition was engendered in Ossie in his boyhood when, after falling from a swing at the age of seven, he suffered severe spinal injuries and was forced to spend over a year in bed. He knew a lot of illness and discomfort in his adolescence, and was not really restored to excellent health until two major operations had been performed in America. So Ossie knew something of suffering and endurance.

Like most young couples Ossie and Megan looked forward to having a family, and anticipated no difficulties for their offspring. Two lovely bright-eyed children were born to them and have grown into lively attractive adults. They did well at school and took up professional training, in law and architecture. Theirs proved a happy home. Ossie thinks that he was not nearly as severe a disciplinarian as his own father. . . .

For this family there have been several memorable occasions during the past ten years. When Ossie had completed twenty-five years with the big company for which he works he was given the customary party and presentation. Nice things were said about him and special references made to his equitable disposition and cheerful smile – his open, warm greeting to everyone is noticeable. There was then the celebration of the couple's silver wedding, when a party was held in the chapel hall, which was full of relatives and friends, and rejoicing was great. At the end of the evening a fine professional photograph of their grown-up children was presented to Ossie and Megan, a picture of a couple of good-looking, assured young people. This is now of course proudly displayed in the parents' sitting-room.

Perhaps the most exciting event in the married life of Ossie and Megan was going to Trinidad in 1979 to visit Ossie's family, something they had not been able to do before. Trinidad is an independent republic off the coast of Venezuala, and is the most southerly of the West Indian islands. Its history has been touched by many cultures – African, Indian, Creole, Syrian, Chinese, European. It is an island with rich natural resources.

After being married for sixteen years, Megan was now going to meet Ossie's relatives, many for the first time, and to take her children to their father's birthplace. She was a little apprehensive, even after all this time; would the family by now be accustomed to the idea of Ossie's European wife and willing to welcome her?

She now says, "There was not need for any worry –

we had the most wonderful welcome." Her eyes shine as she says this.

They had the joy of staying in Ossie's old family home. Megan was sad that she was not able to talk to her parents-in-law at last, and convince them of the happiness she and Ossie and the children shared. Both Ossie's parents were by then dead. "My father was pretty severe", says Ossie, "but he was kind, and both he and my mother were very dignified." Megan could imagine Ossie's boyhood in these cool rooms, the little boy so much of whose childhood had been spent in pain. One day the couple were looking through family papers in a drawer in mother's former bedroom, when out tumbled a photograph album with dozens of snaps of Megan and Ossie and the children. These snaps had obviously been much handed around. "She really was proud of us all", thought Megan with a glad heart.

It was very moving for her to be taken to visit the various members of Ossie's family, brothers and sisters whom she had heard about but whom, for the most part, she had never met. All her husband's tales of his boyhood came to life as they covered the island. There were intimate get-togethers and huge parties, and the children were made much of. They met their cousins for the first time and thoroughly enjoyed themselves. They explored the island – they had heard about the Caroni swamp, roosting place of the scarlet ibis bird, and of the famous seemingly-bottomless pitch lake, renowned for its production of asphalt. They absorbed the life and colour of this exotic place, sometimes known as the "Rainbow country", whose blood ran in their veins.

Best of all, says Megan, were the celebrations at Christmas time, not long after their arrival. This was a Christmas in the burning, spicy air of December. "It seemed so funny", Megan recalls, "to be getting the Christmas tree ready, just as usual, but with artificial snow, and with Christmas day itself being so hot." She is eager to confirm what a marvellous time they all had. "I truly did not want to come back home – it was great."

The young people, as naturally they do, have now quit home for the wider world, leaving Megan and Ossie to continue their peaceful and happy days. All the older parents have gone. Life is busy in this home, and in the responsible life the couple have made for themselves. Megan is a thoughtful Christian woman, who became and remains involved in the nearby small chapel where they were married, and which means so much to them. Despite some years of serious illness, she undertakes the provision of preachers in this little evangelical cause. Ossie plays the organ. They are both involved with a small competent choir and sing together within it. Without thinking too much about it, they show the world how united and successful a mixed marriage can be . . . they are still making music together.

Both Ends of the Family

Families on the whole are not so large as they were in Victorian days. There are fewer uncles and cousins, and not so many "maiden aunts" living usefully alongside the family. Grandparents are still universally popular and valued, though nowadays they tend to have significant lives of their own to a greater extent than in the past. Even the toughest of them speaks with enthusiasm of grandchildren, and there is genuine sorrow when, through some family break-up or through travel difficulties, they cannot see much of their grandchildren.

Children and young people, when asked about their views on family life, are extremely honest. They voice a number of grumbles but usually finally admit that there is "no one like Mum and Dad – and even brothers and sisters". Parents and young adults still waltz around one another, and both allege they cannot understand the other.

Bearing all this in mind, it is amazing how each will stand up for the other when family life comes under threat.

The libertarian aspirations of young adults still continue to worry many parents, but they probably always will.

Honest Words –
Grandfather and Children

With the Queen Mother as perhaps the most famous role-model, Grandparents are usually important in the lives of families. Families are important to the grandparents, as most are quick to agree. Frederick speaks like this: "It is rather special being a grandfather. As an only child and the last of my line, to have two fine grandsons has given me a sense of dynastic security. They have given me some hope of earthly immortality. The real joy, however, is the company of the boys themselves. At Christmas, for example, one recaptures something of one's own childhood, as they excitedly anticipate Christmas morning and, rising early, awaken the whole household as stockings are emptied and parcels explored.

"The years fall away as one finds oneself shouting encouragement as they compete at swimming galas. Then there are the board games, and being soundly beaten at snooker, or trying to keep the peace as umpire in table-cricket. All this adds zest to the gathering years. It takes one's energy but this will be recouped for next time, when again I try to keep up with 'Come on Gramps' and I am again 'one of the boys. . . .'

"These boys have a special place in my prayers, not only that they will grow up to be fine young men, fit in

133

body and mind, but that because they come from a loving and stable home they will be able to withstand the corrupting influences of much modern society. I hope I live long enough to see them well on the road to living good and useful lives. . . ."

Some grandparents have the proverbial quiverful and yet see each child as an individual. The Countess of Longford – Elizabeth – thinks she sees human life repeating itself in her twenty-six grandchildren (fourteen boys and twelve girls – not forgetting three muchloved "steps") for they cover a span of thirty-one years.

Elizabeth says: "The two eldest – girls – have each given me a great-grandchild and an excellent book written by herself. So I like to see in them improved versions of myself; I being a devotee of children and of writing. My youngest grandchild – a boy – can now stump happily round his playpen. Here I seem to note a difference from my own eight children, who all screamed the minute they were penned in. Does it signify a touch of agoraphobia in the next generation? Or perhaps it means that this baby's imagination can create a whole world of teddies and trollies, behind bars? I use the words '*my* grandchildren' without the pricks of conscience that sometimes used to accompany '*my* children'. For I find no danger of possessiveness with these grandchildren. The reasons are obvious: there are too many and they do not, alas, live under my roof. At the same time, their independent lives confer a special grace on the affection they bestow. . . ."

Long before the actual births, grandparents get excited. Two grandmothers say, "Even before an infant is born, the imminent arrival causes far-reaching ripples in the family pool. Next to the new parents and any siblings, the grandparents are probably the most affected by the addition to the family", thinks Joan. And at the actual birth, as Sylvia tells us, "There is joy and delight in noting family features".

Relationships between grandparents and children are usually warm. "There is the excited anticipation on the young children's faces when the grandparents arrive, and the eager expressions when the little ones peer round the bedroom door in the morning in expectation of a romp on the bed", says one obviously popular grandmother, Sylvia. Such a warm relationship is encapsulated simply and basically by Laura, when she says: "There is nothing like the moment when a young grandchild sidles up and puts her arms around my neck and whispers 'I love you Granny'."

Looking out for family likenesses causes interest and sometimes amusement. We have all said, "Oh, isn't so-and-so like Aunty So-and-so" – perhaps in a physical attribute, perhaps in some mannerism, such as the lift of an eyebrow, or the tilt of the head. Laura speaks of one child's "funny toes" which have appeared again after skipping a generation.

Differences of temperament are absorbing to grandparents, good traits usually accepted as descending from their own side of the family. One daughter's child is known as "always the one who starts things and then says innocently – 'It wasn't me'!" Unattractive traits appear sometimes, but are of short duration, as a rule on holiday. "The most trying", says Laura, "is the picky eater – the one you simply can't please."

Most grandparents will be ready to support and admire the demonstrations of grandchildren's skills. Some are loyal beyond the call of duty, as with Sylvia, probably the first to admit that she is not a particularly musical person, but who patiently listens to and applauds recitals from exponents of piano, organ, keyboard, bassoon, clarinet, violin, viola, tuba, flute and drums. . . .

One grandmother is delighted that grandchildren and grandparents can be friends. She recalls her sixteen-year-old granddaughter being asked by her grandfather what she and her gran had been talking about. "Oh, only girly-talk", said the girl airily. "What a boost for a sixty-eight year old", says the Grandmother, "it made my day!"

This Gran, speaking also for her husband, goes on philosophically – "We can admire, fuss and cuddle – but we don't have to endure sleepless nights. We can share and enjoy board-games, toys and books – but not every day. Confidences can be shared and worries too, but grandparents do not have to make the decisions. We have, in short, all the pleasures and few of the worries that come to parents."

And in the happiest of families these relationships continue. Laura, whose grandchildren are of all ages, and who has also several great-grandchildren, keeps in a drawer all the "little things" given to her as gifts throughout the years. There are drawings, birthday and Christmas cards, tiny bits of needlework, a minute china cat, a rather good poem from a seven-year-old, an illustrated story, and even a scrappy page with a "sum" on it – ticked by the teacher. "They speak to me of happy, happy days. . . ."

In some families, these relationships run deep. Some children are brought up by Granny and suffer a lot when the relationship is ended by death. And sometimes the relationship is changed, and Granny becomes the responsibility of a young adult. In one such family situation, a caring grandson was there to sit by his grandmother and hold her hand as she passed peacefully away. . . .

Children, at the other end of the family, are nothing if not honest, particularly very little ones, who do not beat about the bush in describing the best and worst of family relationships. Nicola (10) wishes that her Mum did not work so hard and, with the growing concern of even young children for the environment, doesn't like "to see my family using aerosols which destroy the ozone layer". She is very sure of what she would miss "if I didn't have mum and dad and my sister."

Girls of about ten to fifteen often speak critically of younger brothers, who are apparently "wimps" and "pathetic". One girl, says, "Living with David isn't too bad but he can be very personal . . . sometimes he really gets on my nerves." The scorn of brothers for younger sisters is just as clearly emphasized. Miranda says, "My big brother laughs at me for the magazines I read and the groups I listen to – he really thinks I am stupid . . . but I do like him and I wish he would let me borrow some of his clothes – he has such good dress sense. . . ."

"Arguing" is high on everybody's list of admissions about family life. There is arguing with siblings – "We argue about what to watch on television and what we are going to do at the weekend" and arguing with parents. Karyn says, "I argue with my Mum and Dad quite a lot about things like leaving clothes on the floor, watching television, listening to tapes when I should be doing homework." Several children cheerfully admit "in an argument in our house soon everyone is involved, but it doesn't last long!" "Full-scale rows even", says another child, still laughing. Holidays seem to generate a lot of argument – "by the end of two weeks we will probably have all fallen out." This child concludes sensibly, "Families are all known to have disagreements but we have fun with each other as well."

A teenager sums it up: "After saying all this about family arguments I wouldn't ask for another Mum, Dad or brother because we all love and care for each other in many different ways."

Children are sometimes quite surprisingly appreciative of their parents' efforts to please them. Says one: "My Mum and Dad help me a lot with my school-work, and take me where I have to go for my drama group, and stay up while I'm out at discos. . . ."

Older young people show a lot of insight into domestic situations. Eighteen-year-old Caroline, from a professional home says, "Parents can give the security necessary for a growing child. They are supportive, caring and comfortable. When necessary, I find my parents a great source of helpful and useful advice. I find them easy to communicate with, something essential for an adolescent, particularly when dealing with my friends. . . ." Lucky Caroline!

Jonathan too thinks that "Younger teenagers especially need an occasional steadying hand – otherwise they can grow up to be rather unlikeable!"

Caroline goes on to remind us of the adolescents' struggle for independence. "Parents can be over-protective which results in the child feeling over-whelmed. When going out you get such questions as: Where are you going? Who are you going with? What time will you be back? This is rather irritating because it is a list of restrictions. I sometimes think a parent's wish is to keep the child always sheltered from the outside world. They treat him or her like an infant because they don't want to, or fail to, recognize that their child is growing up." This young woman concludes, "There has to be a balance in the parent-child relationship and in my experience the good points of a family outweigh the bad ones. . . ."

One fifteen-year-old boy puts it bluntly. "A teenager needs room to grow. Claustrophobic, fussy parents do not help, as one feels one cannot move without being watched." This ties in with another youngster's comments that "families are sometimes too close". Says Jonathan, "Somewhere to go and be alone is a common requirement of all people and this applies as well to teenagers." A girl puts it even more plainly: "Families should leave you alone when you have had enough of their company."

Doing things at home is not a frequent admission by children, except as a ground for argument, but Jonathan does make a suggestion which may, he feels, "provoke a few groans among my friends". He thinks it is helpful for any teenager to start to make contributions domestically, perhaps cooking the odd meal or ironing the occasional shirt. "This will prepare us for the big, bad world."

As children adjust to their sexuality there is evidence of a little sadness at the passing of the old group pursuits and relationships. Says Miranda: "When we were little we all used to get on well and do things together. Just lately, as we've been growing up, and I've become more of a 'proper girl', we haven't been quite so close . . . I've been left out of water-fights and things because I'm a girl. . . ." She also recognizes clearly the gradual loosening of sibling and family ties generally – "Family life is nice but as you grow up you tend to spend more time with your friends and less with your family."

The universal struggle of parents to come to terms with their bewildering growing children is well put by Kate who says, laughing, "My dad thinks I should move out and come back when I'm sixteen so that we can all have a break, and perhaps we will all get on better in a few more years." How many parents will echo this sentiment! But Kate touchingly sums up what most children seem to imply:

"At the end of the day I would never swap my Mum, my Dad and my brother for anything else on the assembly line of families. . . ." So say most children of happy families when asked. As David puts it: "Family life is really important, no matter the size of the family or the colour of your skin. . . ."

It Can Happen

There are some families where, on the whole, things seem to go right, and some heads of families who seem to have special skills in keeping families happy. Gifts of temperament and management seem to have been given in special degree to some people. They are very blessed and, in the instance of the story related here, they themselves are a blessing to society. It is not given to all families to be so outgoing and so welcoming as the Buck parents, but it is mighty encouraging to know that such kindly and effective human beings are around. Fortunate have been the young lives nurtured within their shelter.

Look Back In Contentment – The Bucks

In a comfortable old house in an East Anglian village sit two people of mature years. The husband gets up. It is time for one of his voluntary jobs – driving home attenders at the nearby day centre for the disabled and elderly. Tall, upright and well-groomed, he strides out to the garage, a contented-looking man. His wife hears a knock at the door and goes to answer. Who knows, it could be one of the big family to whom she is "Mum" or "Auntie". For though their house is now quiet and orderly, in years past it has rung with the noise and laughter of an amazing family life. Verdun and Kathy Buck have borne their own family, adopted four children and fostered so many that they have virtually lost count. They now say, "It wasn't easy but it was not bad at all and a lot of it was very enjoyable."

The Bucks are a healthy looking couple, their faces serene and unruffled, and fresh-complexioned from the country air. They give no indication of the strenuous and challenging years behind them. The rewards are tangible, mainly when cheerful visitors, including their seven grandchildren, fill the house. But they have the satisfaction of knowing that they have given a true family life to many young people, and have seen families through traumatic times.

Kathy had been a midwife, so the care of young babies was no mystery to her and a love of children was ingrained. Verdun – a family name – was a police officer. He too had an appreciation of the value of family life, and after their marriage in the early 1940s, they took it for granted that children would come into their lives. Their own children were gradually supplemented by adopted siblings, the last of these being a child of mixed race. The adopted children have been happy enough not to want to find out about their natural parents, though matters were explained to them at appropriate moments.

Surely this big energetic family was enough? "Then", says Kathy, "I was invited to foster a child, and from that moment we never looked back." Soon she became used to the telephone call from the Social Worker – "Can you take a child now?" And her answer now explains their reaction then – "Well, you can't say no really, can you?"

In their old house there was plenty of room for more beds, and "just one more" didn't seem too difficult. Most of the children fostered were under five years of age when they arrived, and frequently came because of a time of difficulty in the lives of the natural parents. "They just couldn't cope at the time; there was more muddle than anything, and later the parents would want to forget these difficult periods." But whilst they were happening, it was a huge relief to know that in the home of the Bucks, the children were safe and happy.

"The children called me 'Auntie'," says Kathy. "I never pretended to be their Mother. When I could I used to take them home to their families for the day. I remember once having two sisters at the same time — they were eight and ten, lovely little girls; there was just a temporary problem when the father died. I still hear from them. . . ."

"It must have been terribly hard work" is the first reaction of many people to the Bucks' family life. Kathy agrees and says she could not have managed without the agreement and support of her husband. They never had any paid help in the house, and with several really young children to care for, life must have been tiring. "Well, we didn't have many rules", she says, "but the few rules we did have helped towards the running of the house. The children made their own beds and had to behave properly at mealtimes; I don't like messy table manners. The girls helped a lot, and frankly we didn't worry too much about standards — we all fed properly and the house was clean."

Wasn't it difficult taking in children under stress? Kathy shakes her head. "Not really. One or two of the children were tearaways but mostly it was the parents who were the problem. The boys could be rascals — once I had four at the same time, and what one didn't think of the others did. But we always had great support from the Social Worker."

Food certainly occupied much of Kathy's time. "I sometimes had this terrible nightmare, that of a huge table laid with white plates and nothing on them!" Actually, Kathy indicates, there was no real problem at all. Verdun thinks there was a lot of food around in the country at that time – people had pigs – and they did seem, he says with a smile, "to look after the policeman". The couple recall the gifts of potatoes and other lovely fresh vegetables that came to their door. "We didn't do things by halves, we had huge sacks of potatoes. We were lucky in having a large empty factory at the end of the garden where we could store things. Sometimes we were given a pigeon or a hare, that made it easier. We also had an allotment. None of the children was fussy over food. We used to have two long tables in the big kitchen and everyone could sit down at the same time. The kids used to say 'Don't send the dish down that end, it won't come back!' It was hard work but it never seemed a hardship." Kathy recently talked these days over with a daughter-in-law, and they agreed that it was mindboggling to think of all the food they had prepared for as many as fifteen or sixteen people at a time. "But we always had enough, we used to do masses of potatoes. . . ." Some things were easier then, thinks Kathy, "The butcher from the next village used to call three times a week".

As to the attending to and bringing-up of babies and very young children, the Bucks had a commonsense

147

approach. In a day when the medical emphasis was upon strict discipline in childcare, the Bucks would use the far more relaxed approach now considered sensible. "There were all these baby books about", says Verdun, "but unfortunately the babies hadn't read them!" He does not think he was a very strict disciplinarian but agrees that he "like things to be right". Perhaps having a police officer as a "Dad" or "Uncle" had a certain inhibiting effect on potential wrongdoers . . . There was the usual bit of rebellion among adolescents and the occasional "I'm going to leave home!" "But they never did", says Kathy comfortably, "I think they knew when they were well off." The Bucks agree that living away from towns prevented many problems – there was always plenty of room for "letting off steam", peaceful days relaxing and exploring the countryside, fishing, football, and biking round the lanes, even the little ones on their tricycles seemingly safe as houses. "The older ones seemed more responsible then", muses Verdun. "There wasn't much vandalism or such-like from our lot, or at least nobody came complaining. And we didn't have trouble from other children. I think their fathers said something like, 'Don't you go getting the policeman to call round here – I'll kill you if you do!'" He smiled at the remembrance. Plenty of space seems to have been the key to pacific living. "And if their noise got too much, we retreated into another room, that's the best of a large old house."

The Bucks were asked the big question: "How did your own children by birth relate to all these other children – their adopted siblings and the constant stream of other boys and girls passing through the home?"

"It seemed to work out all right. When we started fostering, one of two of the older ones were at boarding school, and the others thought it was great that they had so many children to play with. We tried to treat all the children the same and not make any difference." It was always painful when a foster-child left, even if there had been difficulties. "But we always felt they had been lent to us, and we always knew that they would be going away and we tried to make it easy."

Individual situations required individual attention. The Bucks went to great lengths to enrich the thinking of their last adopted daughter, a lovely half-Chinese girl. "We talked to her a lot about her Chinese ancestry and tried to encourage her pride in this. We used to take her to 'anything Chinese – exhibitions, etc'." Perhaps partly as a consequence, this young woman later read Chinese at the University and went happily to work in the Far East.

"Some of the best times were holiday times", recalls Kathy. "We never had much money to arrange this, but people were kind and friends often lent us a cottage or flat. For several years we squashed into a fisherman's cottage. And I remember one lovely holiday in Cornwall with six of the children, including one little spastic girl. She was in her pram, and we just stuck this into our old dormobile and away we all went. It was hectic but exciting, with lots of fun, with everyone relaxed and ready to enjoy themselves. Happy memories!"

The Bucks attended the old parish church as a family, and as Kathy says, "I suppose they all took it for granted that we would all go. They were all christened and confirmed. Frankly, there wasn't much else to do on Sunday then . . . but we were all members of the Church of England." And as she points out, it was not far to go, the fine old church being only a few hundred yards away.

Nowadays the Bucks have plenty of quiet and privacy. It can indeed be very quiet in the old house. Happily, a married daughter is very near and the family keeps in touch, especially at Christmas.

Happy families? There's certainly been one in this house and it's good to hear that the tentacles reach out to another generation of happy families too. Of course it may all sound like a rural idyll, but alongside the happy companionship went the bewilderment of the children who came so suddenly into the Buck home; also the relentlessly hard work to make a success of coping with this houseful of young people. But Kathy and Verdun say, "It's been a full life but we wouldn't have had it any different. . . ."

Also available in Fount Paperbacks

Mother Teresa: Her People and Her Work
DESMOND DOIG

'Desmond Doig has written a beautiful book and his writing and the pictures capture Mother Teresa and her people and her work exactly. He understands it. I want to cry, with anger, with passion, with compassion, with sadness at the waste of human life and energy. But no, that is not enough, it is a waste of energy, we must do something to help her.'

Financial Times

Something Beautiful for God
MALCOLM MUGGERIDGE

'For me, Mother Teresa of Calcutta embodies Christian love in action. Her face shines with the love of Christ on which her whole life is centred. *Something Beautiful for God* is about her and the religious order she has instituted.'

Malcolm Muggeridge

A Gift for God
MOTHER TERESA

'This selection of Mother Teresa's sayings, prayers, meditations, letters and addresses on themes of love and compassion . . . touches profound spiritual themes . . . Its size belies its power to inspire and uplift.'

Church of England Newspaper

The Love of Christ
MOTHER TERESA

A further collection of Mother Teresa's writings and sayings, including hitherto unpublished extracts from her retreat addresses to her community of nuns.

'Do not read this book . . . if you do not want . . . to be shaken in conscience and shamed into loving God and other people more.'

Iain Mackenzie, Church Times

Also available in Fount Paperbacks

The Holy Spirit
BILLY GRAHAM

'This is far and away Graham's best book. It bears the stamp of someone who has seen everything, and then has worked painstakingly and carefully in making his own assessment . . . The Christian world will be reading it for many years to come.'

Richard Bewes,
Church of England Newspaper

To Live Again
CATHERINE MARSHALL

The moving story of one woman's heart-rending grief and of her long hard struggle to rediscovery of herself, of life, of hope.

A Man Called Peter
CATHERINE MARSHALL

The story of a brilliantly successful minister and of a dynamic personality. Told by his wife, it is also the story of their life together; a record of love and faith that has few equals in real life.

The Prayers of Peter Marshall
CATHERINE MARSHALL

'This is a truly wonderful book, for these prayers are a man speaking to God – and speaking in a way that involves listening for an answer.'

British Weekly

Also available in Fount Paperbacks

A Gift for God
MOTHER TERESA OF CALCUTTA

'The force of her words is very great . . . the message is always the same, yet always fresh and striking.'

Malcolm Muggeridge

Strength to Love
MARTIN LUTHER KING

'The sermons . . . read easily and reveal a man of great purpose, humility and wisdom . . . in the turbulent context of the American race conflict, Dr King's statements have the ring of social as well as spiritual truth . . .'

Steven Kroll
The Listener

A Book of Comfort
ELIZABETH GOUDGE

'The contents are worth ten of the title: this is a careful, sensitive anthology of the illuminations in prose and verse that have prevented the world from going wholly dark over the centuries.'

Sunday Times

The Desert in the City
CARLO CARRETTO

'. . . we have been in the hands of one of the finest of modern spiritual writers, who helps us on the road of love in Christ.'

Philip Cauvin, the Universe

Also available in Fount Paperbacks

The Mind of St Paul
WILLIAM BARCLAY

'There is a deceptive simplicity about this fine exposition of Pauline thought at once popular and deeply theological. The Hebrew and Greek backgrounds are described and all the main themes are lightly but fully treated.'   *The Yorkshire Post*

The Plain Man Looks at the Beatitudes
WILLIAM BARCLAY

'. . . the author's easy style should render it . . . valuable and acceptable to the ordinary reader.'   *Church Times*

The Plain Man Looks at the Lord's Prayer
WILLIAM BARCLAY

Professor Barclay shows how this prayer that Jesus gave to his disciples is at once a summary of Christian teaching and a pattern for all prayers.

The Plain Man's Guide to Ethics
WILLIAM BARCLAY

The author demonstrates beyond all possible doubt that the Ten Commandments are the most relevant document in the world today and are totally related to mankind's capacity to live and make sense of it all within a Christian context.

Ethics in a Permissive Society
WILLIAM BARCLAY

How do we as Christians deal with such problems as drug taking, the 'pill', alcohol, morality of all kinds, in a society whose members are often ignorant of the Church's teaching? Professor Barclay approaches a difficult and vexed question with his usual humanity and clarity, asking what Christ himself would say or do in our world today.

Also available in Fount Paperbacks

BOOKS BY C. S. LEWIS

Fern-Seed and Elephants

'The magic of his writings shows no abatement . . . the final essay alone makes the paperback worth its weight in gold . . . a substantial and most helpful analysis of the doctrines of the end of the world and the final judgement.'

R. L. Roberts, Church Times

The Screwtape Letters

'Excellent, hard-hitting, challenging, provoking.'

The Observer

Screwtape Proposes a Toast

Screwtape appears again but this time to propose a toast at a diabolical banquet. These essays are witty, original, outspoken, offering abundant and delightful nourishment to the half-starved Christian imagination of our time.

Till We Have Faces

'An imaginative retelling of the myth of Cupid and Psyche, with Christian overtones, to which the author brings his customary clarity of thought and superlative story-telling powers.'

British Weekly

Fount Paperbacks

Fount is one of the leading paperback publishers of religious books and below are some of its recent titles.

- ☐ PAUL THE INTERPRETER George Appleton £2.95
- ☐ ACTING AS FRIENDS Michael De-la-Noy £4.50
- ☐ THE BURNING BUSH John Drury £2.99
- ☐ A KEY TO THE OLD TESTAMENT
  David Edwards £3.50
- ☐ THE CRY OF THE SPIRIT Tatiana Goricheva £3.99
- ☐ CROSSFIRE Richard Holloway £3.50
- ☐ CREATION Martin Israel £2.99
- ☐ BEING IN LOVE William Johnston £3.50
- ☐ THE MASS J. M. Lustiger £2.99
- ☐ CALLED TO HOLINESS Ralph Martin £2.95
- ☐ THE HIDDEN JOURNEY Melvyn Matthews £3.50
- ☐ REFLECTIONS ON MY WORK Thomas Merton £3.99
- ☐ DEATH BE NOT PROUD Peter Mullen £2.99
- ☐ SCRIPTURE PROMISES Carmen Rojas £3.50
- ☐ LIGHT AND LIFE Grazyna Sikorska £2.95
- ☐ EASTER GARDEN Nicola Slee £3.95
- ☐ CHRISTMAS – AND ALWAYS Rita Snowden £2.99
- ☐ CELEBRATION Margaret Spufford £2.95

All Fount Paperbacks are available at your bookshop or newsagent, or they can be ordered by post from Fount Paperbacks, Cash Sales Department, G.P.O. Box 29, Douglas, Isle of Man. Please send purchase price plus 22p per book, maximum postage £3. Customers outside the UK send purchase price, plus 22p per book. Cheque, postal order or money order. No currency.

NAME (Block letters) _____

ADDRESS_____

_____

_____